DAVENPORT'S NEVADA WILLS AND ESTATE PLANNING LEGAL FORMS

WRITTEN BY
ALEX RUSSELL AND ROBERT MAXWELL

DAVENPORT'S NEVADA WILLS AND ESTATE PLANNING LEGAL FORMS

written by attorneys
Alex Russell and Robert Maxwell

PUBLICATION DATA

(informal, library may use different data)

Names: Russell, Alex, 1972- author ; Maxwell, Robert, 1960- author

Title: Davenport's Nevada Wills And Estate Planning Legal Forms

Other Titles: Davenport's Wills

Description: Davenport Publishing 2023

Suggested Identifiers: 9798391812234, LCCN 2021909030, 9798748423373

Subjects: LCSH: Wills--United States;
Wills--United States--Forms;
Estate Planning--United States;
Legal Forms

Classification: LFF KF755 .C55 2022 (or as library chooses)
DDC 346.73 Rus--dc23 (or as library chooses)

9 8 7 6 5 4 3 2 1 0 0 0 0 0 2 3

WARNING

THIS PUBLICATION IS NOT A SUBSTITUTE FOR LEGAL ADVICE. Publisher and authors say and warn this publication is not giving any legal, accounting, or other professional services or advice, which if wanted can be obtained by consulting in person an attorney or some other professional. **No attorney-client relationship or any relationship creating a duty or obligation is agreed to or created by the purchase or use of this publication or forms.**

CHAPTER 1
BOOK BASICS AND LIST OF FORMS

ESTATE PLANNING CONTROLS THINGS IF LATER ABSENT, SICK, OR DEAD

From Davenport Publishing and written by attorneys this book is on "Estate Planning", about doing legal documents to control health care, property, money, children, funeral, and more if later absent, sick, or dead. People have a legal right to control their health care, property, money, and family issues, and so judges, doctors, and others mostly just ask: **"Based on what a person wrote what did they likely want done?"**

ESTATE PLANNING MOSTLY IS DOING SIMPLE THINGS IN 3 AREAS

Estate Planning is mostly doing simple things in 3 areas: <u>After Death</u>, <u>Health Care</u>, and <u>Giving Power</u>. There are 11 ready to use legal forms for Nevada in this book. <u>Many people use just 1 to 3 legal forms</u>.

AFTER DEATH FORMS

<u>**Form 1. Will (Standard)**</u> – a Will (also called a "Last Will And Testament") lets person control things after their death like who gets their money and property, who is Executor, and allowing helpful legal options later.

<u>**Form 2. Will (Guardian)**</u> – Will with part added to name someone as Guardian to care for a minor child under 18 if later needed (like if later no parent is available) and also manage a child's money and property.

<u>**Form 3. Handwritten Will**</u> – this Will skips the usual need for 2 witnesses which saves time and work, but it must be all handwritten by person doing the Will (so no use of typing, computers, or legal forms).

<u>**Form 4. Self-Proving Affidavit**</u> – form <u>sometimes</u> done with a Will to later prove it was properly signed.

<u>**Form 5. Tangible Personal Property List**</u> – lets person easily outside Will write some more gifts to occur after death of tangible personal property like furniture, jewelry, vehicles, art, electronics, tools, and clothes.

HEALTH CARE FORMS

<u>**Form 6. Durable Power Of Attorney For Health Care**</u> – this popular form lets a person be named as Health Care Agent to if needed control health care and also lets health care instructions be written.

<u>**Form 7. Living Will Declaration**</u> – lets a person do serious act of saying stop most health care <u>if later</u> they are incapacitated and doctors think the health situation is very bad and more care likely won't help.

<u>**Form 8. Do-Not-Resuscitate**</u> – does serious act of saying <u>from now on</u> don't try resuscitation to help breathing or heart like C.P.R. (cardio-pulmonary resuscitation), and form is short so can be read quickly.

GIVING POWER FORMS

<u>**Form 9. Statutory Form Power Of Attorney**</u> – lets power over money, property, and more be given to a person like spouse, adult child, or friend so they can do things like use accounts, get records, and sell things.

<u>**Form 10. Temporary Guardian**</u> – lets parent of a child under age 18 give someone power over the child so they can make decisions about health care, school, home, and more if needed.

<u>**Form 11. Affidavit Authorizing Person To Order Burial Or Cremation**</u> – lets a person to later control their dead body give someone power over burial, cremation, and related things and write some suggestions.

NEVADA ESTATE PLANNING LAW APPLIES TO MOST PEOPLE IN NEVADA

This book is for Nevada only. Estate Planning law and legal documents are a bit different in each state. Whether local Estate Planning law applies is based on primary residence of a person (often called "domicile"). Many judges say residence occurs if a person lives in a place and for a moment has no clear plans to leave. Later plans to move don't matter till people actually move. People can stay under a state's Estate Planning laws even if they leave a state if their living elsewhere is temporary and always have very firm plans to return. For example some people who leave for years for travel, for school, for special work projects, and for the military may qualify to keep ties to their old state. Immigrants of any kind can do normal Estate Planning. For health care people often do legal documents to match the state that a hospital or other health facility is in.

BOOK IS SHORT, HAS FORMS TO QUICKLY SEE, AND USES EMPHASIS

This book is short and may read rough but can be read fast. Long books tend to lead to misunderstanding of the basics and skimming. The book has many legal forms people can quickly see. For emphasis some paragraph titles, underlining, and boxes are used. This book capitalizes words like Will, Testator, and Agent but this is optional. To save space some small words are skipped and end quote marks put before punctuation.

LEGAL FORMS CAN HELP AND THIS BOOK PROVIDES "STANDARD FORMS"

Studies on Estate Planning show a surprising 60% of adults have not done anything, 19% used a lawyer for this, and 21% used legal forms. Legal forms are good at most things involved in Estate Planning and can make binding legal documents that judges, doctors, families, banks, and others legally must follow. Also, often a hospital, state agency, charity, or state legislature has made a form most people use and call the "standard form", and doctors, judges, and others may not like to follow different forms. This book does use a standard form in an area if it exists or provides a suitable form. Lawyers often write their own forms.

THIS BOOK COVERS MAJOR LEGAL IDEAS AND SHOULD SUIT MOST PEOPLE

This book covers the main U.S. legal ideas on Estate Planning and most ways Nevada law is different. This book and its forms can't cover every issue that matters to everyone but should suit people without any strange situations or wishes about Estate Planning, which is likely most adults (maybe well over 80%). Strange situations or wishes that may need more research or a lawyer include: a) unusual wishes for gifts, b) wealth over $5 million, c) big medical concerns including extreme age, d) property or money going to a person with disability or special needs, and e) wish to move or hide assets to qualify for government help.

ESTATE PLANNING OFTEN IS NOT VITAL AND INSURANCE MAY HELP MORE

Estate Planning is often not vital and worth much time or money, and may not affect costs, delays, work, and other things as much as thought. For young adults and parents the benefits seem low since only about 9% of people die by 60, and only about 0.13% of children under 18 had 2 parents die to need big legal help. *Social Security Tables: Felicitie Bell*; *Census Life Factors Mortality Study #288*. A lawyer can be used for Estate Planning but they can cost $1000s, take months of work, and make mistakes. In life people weigh costs, benefits, and risks and often go with a low cost option. Life insurance may help more than Estate Planning, and many people pay yearly for $100,000 term life without exam ("simplified issue") after finding a good price.

CHAPTER 2
TERMS, PROPERTY LAW, AND HELPFUL INFORMATION FORM

THERE ARE BASIC TERMS AND IDEAS IN ESTATE PLANNING

Some terms and ideas are basic to Estate Planning.

• "Estate Planning" is people doing legal documents to control things if later absent, sick, or dead. After a document is signed people are usually still free to sell or transfer property, instruct doctors, or change forms. If people choose to sign a legal document in a language they don't know it is usually still valid.

• A "Will" or "will" (this book uses upper case "W") is a legal document done to control issues after death. The phrase "Last Will And Testament" is used since a "Testament" long ago was a small document done along with a Will to do some things. If a person has no valid Will they are described as being "intestate".

• A person who died is called the "decedent" or "deceased". A person getting money or property can be called a "recipient", "beneficiary", or if related to the old owner they are called an "heir" (they "inherit"). The term "survive" or "surviving" means a person is alive after another person has died.

• Someone picked by a person to do things after their death is called by most people and this book as an "Executor", though Nevada in official papers now mostly uses the term "Personal Representative" for this.

• A person doing a Will is called "Testator" or "Will maker". Before about 1990 a woman Testator was called a "Testatrix" and woman Executor called an "Executrix" but this is no longer often done.

• "Probate" is a legal process to do things after death like transfer property, authorize Guardian, and handle creditors. Due to changes in law probate is often "informal" and less costly but can be a hassle for months.

• The "estate" is both a) all property and money of a person that at their death did not automatically transfer to other owners, and b) the entity run by an Executor several months to hold items and do things (sort of like a small corporation). For example accounts may be renamed, like: "Estate of John Smith (deceased)".

• Property is: 1) "real property" (land and buildings), 2) "fixtures" (things tied to real property like fences and wired-in appliances), or 3) "personal property" (everything else like clothes, cars, cash, and accounts).

• Legal documents to control health care things are often called "Advanced Directives", but names vary.

• A person under 18 is called a "minor" and a parent or "Guardian" mostly acts for them. A person not reasonably able to wisely decide things lacks "capacity" and is "incapacitated".

• Documents giving power to someone are often called "Power of Attorney" forms, where the person doing the form called the "Principal" gives power to someone called the "Attorney-in-Fact" or "Agent".

• State law is the "Nevada Revised Statutes". A law is often called a statute or section sometimes shown by an "s" or "§". One example on how to refer to an Nevada law is: "N.R.S. 133.040". A legal form that the legislature wrote into state law for people to find and use if wanted is called a "statutory form".

LEGAL DOCUMENTS MAY NEED TO BE "WITNESSED" OR "NOTARIZED"

A person "doing a legal document" or "doing a form" means filling out and properly signing a document. Some documents to be valid need to be "witnessed" which means someone sees the person doing the form sign and then signs too. Some documents need to be "notarized" which mean a person who is a "notary" ("notary public") sees it signed and then uses an ink stamp and signs too. Notaries with time to help can be found by phoning ahead, and some are at libraries, courts, banks, insurance agents, and mail or copy stores.

ANYONE CAN FILL IN MOST OF A FORM, AND LATER TRY TO KEEP ORIGINAL

When filling out a form except for certain special forms and except for signatures other parts can be filled in by a person not doing the form for themselves. After a legal form is completed and signed usually people try to keep the original and hand out copies but situations vary. Some people do "multiple originals" by having everyone sign identical documents to have many pages with real ink signatures but this can be confusing.

PROBABLY DO NEW FORMS IF DIVORCE, MARRY, HAVE CHILD, OR MOVE

It is recommended people re-do legal documents if they divorce, marry, or a child is born or adopted. To help most states say a Will from another state is still valid after a move but this is not always certain.

"INTESTATE" LAW SAYS WHERE THINGS GO AT DEATH IF THERE IS NO WILL

Nevada "intestate law" says where a dead person's property and money goes if there is no valid Will. This is found in state law starting at N.R.S. 134.010. Some people prefer intestate law and skip doing a Will. The law treats "separate property" and "community property" differently, and this book covers these terms when covering marriage. Note, in some cases a person's grandchild stands in place of their dead parent. Basically, intestate law distributes things based on what surviving (living) family a person left, and says:

• if spouse and 1 child are living, spouse gets community property and separate property is split 1/2 and 1/2,

• if spouse and multiple children (including adopted children) are living, spouse gets community property and 1/3 of separate property and children get 2/3 of separate property,

• if spouse and 1 or 2 parents are living but no children, the spouse gets all community property and 1/2 of separate property and the parent/s get 1/2 of separate property,

• if spouse and brothers/sisters are living but no children and no parents, the spouse gets all community property and 1/2 of separate property and the brothers/sisters gets 1/2 of separate property,

• if some children are living but no spouse, the children get all,

• if some parents are living but no spouse or children, then parents get all,

• if some brothers/sisters are living but no spouse, children, or parents, then brothers/sisters get all,

• if there is no living spouse, children, parents, and brothers/sisters, then more distant living family get things and if no such family exist it goes to the State of Nevada (it "escheats", which is very rare).

PEOPLE SHOULD DETERMINE WHAT THEY OWN SO CAN GIFT OR TRANSFER

People can only gift or transfer by Will and other ways things they own, so people should research what they own. By law a person usually owns all they earn as wages and salary, their share of income and profit tied to property they own, and owns or partly owns most things their money or property buys or improves.

4

For items with "title" documents (real estate or vehicles) or where there is a "listed owner" (like accounts and various investments) the named persons are usually the owners unless evidence shows special facts. As this book says later married people often share 50/50 ownership of most things in Community Property law states like Nevada. A person during life can sell property, make gifts, or transfer items even if items are named in a Will, so maybe should consider if they already sold or gave away property they name in a Will gift.

THINGS OWNED IN SPECIAL WAYS MAY LIMIT GIFTING

A person should consider if they own real estate or other property in special ways which may limit gifting by Will and other ways. Laws in states vary but some special ways of ownership or property are:

a) "joint tenant with right of survivorship" or similar set up by paperwork, so at a death property transfers automatically to other named owners regardless of a Will, which often is how the family house is held,

b) papers say a "life estate" exists, so then if life of someone ends the other people in papers get item, and

c) "Trust property" occurs if paperwork made a Trust entity and property was transferred into it, so then at or after a death the Trust papers tell a Trustee where to transfer such property.

Normal jointly owned property <u>can</u> be gifted by Will, like "I give my half of boat to Kenneth Gregory Smith". Joint ownership can come from agreement, buying with funds from many, or if a gift was to many people.

WARNING: "NON-PROBATE PROPERTY" TRANSFERS IGNORE ANY WILL

Money or property that for some reason automatically transfers on death or soon after to new owners is called "non-probate property". Examples are: a) if a "designated beneficiary" form was done to name persons to at a death get account or investment, b) transfer-on-death account, and c) real property like a house held by 2 people as "joint tenants with survivorship" or similar so at a death the survivor gets things. Insurance with a beneficiary also usually ignores a Will. Trying to do non-probate transfers for all things is called "avoiding probate", but it is rare as it may make living and paperwork a hassle for years, benefits are small, and it is hard to not miss an item and fail. <u>People should consider non-probate transfers that will occur automatically on death and consider what property and money will be left to transfer by Will.</u>

SOME LESS COMMON AND LESS USEFUL FORMS ARE NOT IN THIS BOOK

This book skips some less common or less useful documents.

• A "Codicil" can modify a Will but it is easier and legally safer to just re-do a Will.

• Some people do a "Revocable Living Trust" so Trust entity with Trustee holds property or money during their life however long, usually done to after death avoid small delay, costs, or work (by "avoiding probate"). This is rare as it requires immediately moving most of a person's things into a Trust causing maybe years of hassles, mostly for small benefits for people who are probably happy to later do work to get things by Will.

• "Childrens Trust" papers can be done maybe in a Will so a Trust at a death gets money or property for a minor child to manage until 18, but this is uncommon due to possible cost and hassles, since it rarely matters (as this book explains), and since most Wills already arrange other legal help for young children.

• Some people do a "Pet Trust" to help a pet, but it's easier to just give money in Will to person given a pet.

SOME PEOPLE DO "HELPFUL INFORMATION" FORM

Some people do <u>a "Helpful Information" form that lawyers write so family or friends after their death have more information</u> about things. Often people staple records or lists to this. <u>See next pages.</u>

ESTATE PLANNING HELPFUL INFORMATION

For more space attach copies of form or blank pages. Keep pages by Will or other place for Executor or family.

1. Personal Information (Name, Birthdate, Social Security #, special family details, other):

2. Real estate, vehicles, and other major tangible property (especially if people may not find them):

3. Non-tangible assets like stocks, accounts, investments, loans owed you, and business interests:

4. Possible income or insurance like pensions, retirement, disability, insurance, or contracts:

5. Debts owed by you like credit card, loan, student loan, mortgage, vehicle loan, and accounts payable:

6. Names and information of professionals used (attorneys, accountants, brokers, doctors, others):

7. Computer passwords and helpful files, document places, and safes or safe-deposit boxes codes/keys:

8. Other helpful things, wishes for funeral, special requests, and any last messages to family and friends:

CHAPTER 3
WILL BASICS

WILL LETS "TESTATOR" CONTROL SOME THINGS AFTER DEATH

A Will is done by a person to control things after their death. A person doing a Will is called "Testator" or "Will maker". Usually a Testator <u>when signing</u> must be at least 18 years old, of sound mind (rational with sufficient memory), and not be under duress (unfair pressure or threat). Most people can do a Will. Saying or even writing about things to occur at or after death often is ineffective if not written in a Will. If people choose to sign a legal document like a Will in a language they don't know it is usually still valid.

USUALLY SIGN WILL IN FRONT OF 2 WITNESSES WHO THEN SIGN

USUALLY A WILL TO BE VALID MUST BE WRITTEN AND HAVE 2 WITNESSES

Usually to be a valid Nevada Will a document must a) show it is meant as a Will, b) be written, and c) be signed in front of 2 witnesses. Usually a Will must be on paper so a "Video Will" or "Audio Will" has no legal effect. Nevada now allows "Electronic Wills" signed electronically and remotely, but these are harder to do and few people use these. Note, as this book explains later Nevada like about half the states does let a person skip using the normal 2 witnesses if the Will is all handwritten by person doing the Will.

WITNESSES SHOULD BE AT LEAST 18 AND NOT GETTING WILL GIFTS

<u>A person to act as witness must be at least age 18</u>. It is not required but preferable a witness not be old or live far away. Under Nevada law a person named to get something in a Will <u>is</u> a valid witness, but any Will gifts to them are void so won't later be carried out. The only exception is if there are 2 other competent witnesses. To avoid this problem many people use witnesses who are not named at all in any Will gift. Most people also try to not use as a witness a person named in a Will as Executor, Guardian, or similar. Often used as witnesses are neighbors, friends, workers at a business, strangers, or more distant family.

TESTATOR AND 2 WITNESSES SIGN A WILL WHEN TOGETHER IN 1 ROOM

To complete a Will usually Testator signs in front of 2 witnesses who then also sign. Everyone should be in 1 room and see each person sign. Witnesses usually read just the 1 paragraph they sign and not more. Witnesses and Testator showing each other an ID with their name on it is not required but is common. Testator need not initial Will pages. A Testator or witness should use their full legal name unless they dislike it and rarely use it. A person who can't move a hand to sign a Will should consult with a lawyer to do a Will. Nevada law does <u>not</u> require witnesses to a Will know or be told what it is. Though not required often a Testator tells witnesses a thing like, "My name is _____ and this is the Will I want and do voluntarily and want you 2 people to witness". Some Testators also chat with witnesses a few minutes to show they are rational.

KEEP SIGNED WILL IN A SAFE PLACE IT CAN BE FOUND AFTER A DEATH

People should keep a Will so it can be found within weeks of their death, like in desk, drawer, safe, or safe deposit box. It can be given to a person to hold. It may help to tell people where to find a Will and any needed code or keys. Most Nevada courts will not accept a Will for safekeeping before the Testator dies.

CANCELING OLD WILLS IS USUALLY NOT A PROBLEM

Revoking (canceling) old Wills is usually not a problem. New Wills often say old Wills are revoked, and all Will forms in this book say this. To revoke a Will a person can also write "void" or "canceled" or "X" on a Will. Crossing out just part of a Will usually has no effect, and revoking a Will usually doesn't revive an old Will.

MOST WILLS SAY SKIP ANY "BOND" AND ALLOW "INFORMAL" PROBATE

Most Wills say no "bond" or "surety" is needed for the Executor. Most people do not this since this is costly insurance against misconduct paid with estate money and most people trust the people they named. To help most Wills also authorize "informal probate" which is a legal option to reduce some costs and delays. Usually probate is not too slow with 1 year common but for small estates quicker legal options are available. Usually probate is not too costly and after expenses often over 95% of value gets to wanted persons.

MOST WILLS HAVE MISCELLANEOUS PART TO HELP AVOID LEGAL ISSUES

Most Wills have a "Miscellaneous" part with paragraphs of legal language to avoid some legal problems.

WILL CAN NAME AN EXECUTOR TO DO THINGS AFTER A DEATH

CAN NAME PERSON "EXECUTOR" TO HAVE POWER TO ACT AFTER A DEATH

Most people in a Will name someone as "Executor" to do things after their death. State law gives an Executor power to do things, like transfer property or money to new owners, handle creditors, and do probate. Most Wills have words to give Executor further power. Often Executor is a spouse, family member, or friend. If needed a judge can always name someone to do this job, but family may argue about who exactly to pick. A lawyer or bank can be Executor if they agree and get a large fee. Naming 2 people to both be Executor is allowed but rare due to risk of disagreements and delay, and since any 1 person named should be trusted. Note, in Nevada the term "Personal Representative" is now often used in Wills and official legal papers for the person handling things after a death, but most people and this book mostly use the old term Executor.

EXECUTOR CAN BE PAID AND ESTATE PAYS FOR EXPENSES AND COSTS

A Nevada law has a fee schedule to pay Executor for their work about 3% of the estate after deductions for mortgages and liens, and most people find this fair. But often Executors skip asking for pay to not owe income tax and to leave more money in the estate to carry out Will gifts. There is an optional fee schedule for a lawyer hired to help with probate, but many people and this book's Will forms just say to pay a lawyer a smaller hourly fee. Money an Executor or estate needs for things like repairs, insurance, costs, utilities, fees, and lawyer is gotten from estate accounts or selling property. People named as Executor can get Will gifts.

EXECUTOR IS PERSON AT LEAST 18

A person to be Executor must be age 18 or older and have no felony criminal record. The person need not be a Nevada resident or even a U.S. citizen, but being local can make their later work far easier to do. A judge may later remove or block someone who seems very unsuitable or does a very bad job as Executor. Some people in a Will name a 2nd person to be Executor if the 1st person is unavailable, like by adding: "or if they are reasonably unable to serve I name _____ to serve". But most people skip this since it's rarely needed, if a problem is seen a new Will can be done, or a judge can always just pick someone.

CHAPTER 4
WILL GIFTS INCLUDING RESIDUE

MAIN USE OF WILL IS TO SAY GIFTS TO HAPPEN AFTER DEATH

People use a Will mostly to say what happens to their property and money after their death, usually by making various Will gifts. Verbal and even written statements about this are not usually valid if not in a Will. A Will can control property acquired after it was signed.

WILL GIFTS USING SIMPLE WORDS IS BEST AND CAN BE A BIT UNCERTAIN

Making gifts in a Will using simple words is often best, using words like "I give to" and "I gift to". This is legally fine and avoids confusing legal words like "bequest", "devise", and "legacy" which few people know. The basic legal rule is <u>a Will gift is sufficiently detailed if people who knew Testator can inform Executor or a judge what Testator meant more likely than not</u>, and certainty is <u>not</u> needed to carry out a Will gift.

PEOPLE ARE MOSTLY FREE TO GIFT THEIR THINGS AS WANTED

A person is mostly free to say what happens to their money and property after their death. This book does explain some limited rights to decedent's things any spouse, children under age 18, and creditors have.

IN WILL CAN DO "SPECIFIC GIFTS" TO GIFT PARTICULAR PROPERTY

Most Wills have "specific gifts" to give <u>particular things</u>. Specific gifts can be any property, like "I give ax to Ed Blom" and "I give UBank account #84548573 to Sue Wu". If a gift is not clear the law assumes all of a kind of thing is given, like "I give jewelry to Ann Po" means <u>all</u> jewelry. But gifting specific property can have surprises like value of an item can change, or a Will gift may not occur later if property is no longer owned.

IN WILL CAN DO "GENERAL GIFTS" LIKE OF MONEY

Wills can do "general gifts" where what is gifted is not particular property but can be flexibly chosen, like "I give 1 of my 3 cars to Ed Po" which lets an Executor pick which car. The usual general gift is money, like "I give $5 to Ed Vu". Money gifts are easy to write, let equal gifts be made, and are safer since specific items might not be owned at death. To carry out money gifts an Executor uses accounts or sells some property.

LATER DIVORCE OR MURDER CANCELS WILL GIFTS TO A PERSON

Nevada law says a person divorcing or murdering Testator usually cancels all Will gifts to the person.

"RESIDUE CLAUSE" IS CATCH-ALL THAT HELPFULLY GIFTS ANYTHING LEFT

Most Wills by their end have a Residue Clause to gift property or money not gifted or used in Will or other ways, often called a "catch-all" or "left-over" clause. <u>The Residue Clause is covered later in this Chapter</u>.

PERSON IN WILL GIFT USUALLY MUST SURVIVE OR GIFT DOES NOT OCCUR

Many Wills like this book's Will forms say a person named in Will gift must survive (live past) Testator for the gift to occur at all unless gift language says different. If survival is not clearly required for a Will gift then what then occurs if a named recipient is dead can be unclear (like due to confusing state "anti-lapse" laws). <u>People doing a Will should consider how Will gifts to people dying before Testator usually have no effect</u>. Many people if they see person in a Will gift has died re-do a Will or trust the Residue Clause to handle it.

CAN ADD GIFT "ALTERNATE BENEFICIARY" MAYBE FOR SPECIAL ITEMS

A person named in a Will gift dying before a Testator is rare, and if seen most people just re-do a Will or let the Will Residue Clause handle it. But some people to prepare for this small chance maybe for special items add a Will gift an alternate beneficiary, like "I give boat to Ed Wu but if they don't survive me to Ann Wu".

WILL CAN SAY IF RECIPIENT DIES A GIFT GOES TO "LINEAL DESCENDANTS"

A Will gift can say it goes to a person but if they don't survive then to their "lineal descendants per stirpes". Descendants are a person's children and grandchildren. "Per stirpes" is about "how" to spread things and means "by branch", and basically if used this tries to divide things so each family branch gets an equal share. Most Wills use "lineal descendants" language in a Residue Clause. An example shows how it works:

A Will may say: **"Clothes to Sue Wu but if they don't survive to their lineal descendants per stirpes"**, and this means if Sue Wu died and her son Ken Wu is living and her other son Ben Wu has died but left 2 children then, legally, under the law Ken Wu himself gets 50% and Ben Wu's 2 children each get 25%.

PROPERTY OR MONEY IN A "JOINT GIFT" GOES TO MULTIPLE PEOPLE

The same property or money can go to multiple people to each get a part interest, and this is a "joint gift", like "I give boat and all hats to Ann Wu and Sue Han" means each person owns 50% of every item. People later can split things by agreement or as Executor suggests, or Executor can sell items and split the money. If a person in a joint gift has died their part of things usually is left to transfer under a Residue Clause.

GIFT BENEFICIARIES CAN GET PERCENTAGE RATHER THAN EQUAL SHARE

If a Will gift goes to multiple people the law assumes equal shares, but if wanted percentages can be put to make unequal gifts, like "I give boat 90% to Ed Wu and 10% to Joe Hud".

CONDITIONS ON WILL GIFTS ARE RARE DUE TO POSSIBLE PROBLEMS

Putting conditions on a gift, like "I give Ann Poe $90 if she graduates college", can cause problems like years of delay, risk of lawsuits, and big attorneys fees, and due to this conditions are rarely put on Will gifts.

"JOINT WILL" TO RESTRICT SPOUSES TO ONLY GIVE TO CHILDREN IS RARE

A "Joint Will" or similar "Contract To Make A Will" by a lawyer a married couple can sign can bar later Will changes that gift to anyone except children or a spouse. Doing this is rare and can have legal issues.

IN NEVADA "GIFT LISTS" CAN BE USED

This book later shows how state law lets "Gift Lists" give some tangible personal property outside a Will.

AFTER A DEATH FAMILIES OFTEN LET PEOPLE TAKE ITEMS UNOFFICIALLY

After a death many families if no one objects often unofficially let people take small items in ways a dead person mentioned, wrote on notes, put on stickers, or would have wanted, and this usually is not a problem.

NO FEDERAL OR NEVADA TAX IS USUALLY OWED DUE TO A DEATH

Usually no tax is owed as a result of a death, including no inheritance, estate, death, or similar taxes. This is because the "Federal Estate And Gift Tax" only starts when a tax credit is used up covering $12.92 million per person in 2023. The state of Nevada no longer has inheritance, estate, death, or similar taxes.

CAN LEAVE SOME WILL GIFT LINES BLANK OR WRITE THINGS LIKE "SKIPPED"

A person writing a Will can choose to not use some gifts lines in a Will legal form, like by just leaving them blank, writing things like "SKIPPED" or "NONE" in them, or using a computer to delete some gift lines.

RESIDUE CLAUSE GIFTING ALL LEFT IS MAIN WAY USED TO GIFT THINGS

THE "RESIDUE CLAUSE" IS CATCH-ALL THAT HELPS GIFT ANYTHING LEFT

Most Wills by their end have a Residue Clause to gift any property or money not gifted earlier in a Will or used in other ways. Things transferred this way is called the "Residue". Many people gift most their money and property this way by intentionally not mentioning in a Will most things so the Residue Clause handles it. This skips need to describe things and has less legal risk. Later after applying a Residue Clause if anything is left (which is rare) then closest heirs get things (this is closest family).

USUAL RESIDUE CLAUSE HAS 2 PARTS

A short 2 part Residue Clause is usual and is used in this book's Wills, and it has:

1) 1st space to name 1 or more persons to get things if they survive Testator (many name a spouse or closest family here), and if several people are named but only some survive then survivors split things, and

2) 2nd space to name persons to get things if all in 1st space don't survive (so these are fallbacks) (many name next family or friends here), and if a person in 2nd space died their descendants get their share.

EXAMPLE OF 2 PART RESIDUE CLAUSE:

"RESIDUE CLAUSE: I give money and property not gifted earlier:

A) to _____ my husband John Paul Doe _____ if they survive me, then

B) to _____ Sam Doe my son, Beth Wu my daughter, and Greta Fisher my friend _____ and if any of those just named do not survive me their part goes to their lineal descendants, per stirpes."

In this example if John Paul Doe has survived then he gets all things, but if John Paul Doe hasn't survived and also Sam Doe hasn't survived and he left 2 daughters then those 2 daughters split the 1/3 share of Sam Doe so get 1/6 each and other 2 persons in second part Beth Wu and Greta Fisher get 1/3 each.

A FEW PEOPLE RE-WRITE A RESIDUE CLAUSE TO HAVE 1 PART

A normal Residue Clause of 2 parts is often fine and basically person put in 1st part usually gets things. A small fraction of people may want to modify a Will to have a "1 Part Residue Clause" which may gift to a group more equally. People with no spouse and no children are likelier to do this change, but even they often don't bother and just use this book's Will forms as is. See Example below for exact words to use if people want this change to a 1 Part Residue Clause.

EXAMPLE OF 1 PART RESIDUE CLAUSE:

"RESIDUE CLAUSE: The rest, residue, and remainder of my estate, property of any kind and nature, and anything I have an interest in, I give to _Adam Doe and Beth Wu_ who survive me, and to lineal descendants per stirpes of any person just named who did not survive me."

In this example if Adam hasn't survived but had 2 children they each get 25%, and if Beth Wu survived she gets 50%. Or if Beth Wu also hadn't survived and had 5 kids they split her part and each gets 10%.

MUST SUFFICIENTLY DESCRIBE NAMES AND PROPERTY IN WILL GIFTS

PUTTING NAMES OF PEOPLE OR GROUPS IN WILL GIFTS IS FAIRLY EASY

Names in Wills are fairly easy. A judge and Executor assume a person gifts to people they know so it's OK to use common names unless 2 friends or family have the same name. Details can be used if names may not be recognized or to be friendly, like "I give $5 to maid Sue Hill" and "I give $5 to my loyal friend Ed Blum". If people used a nickname "also known as" or "a/k/a" may help, like "I give $5 to Ed Wu a/k/a Old Fishy". Gifts can go to a charity, government, or group, like "I give $5 to The Salvation Army, "I give $5 to Sparks City Library", and "I give all clothes to Bethel Church in Irving, TX". People often phone to get a charity's name.

DESCRIPTIONS OF ITEMS IN WILL GIFTS IS FAIRLY EASY

Describing items in Wills is fairly easy since people rarely own similar items, so probably fine is "I give ax to Ed Wu" and "I give big table to Don Ho". It's OK to gift by list or category, like "I give cow, van, and TV to Ann Vix" or "I give tools to Ed Wu". Financial assets can use plain words like "bank accounts" or "stocks" but details can help, like "UBank account ending #2511". Using item location in a Will gift is a bit risky since a judge may cancel a Will gift if it seems items were placed to affect gifting and not an independent life reason. So, "I give Ed Po items in safe and desk" a judge may not follow, but "I give Ed Po hats at cabin" likely is OK.

GIFTING REAL PROPERTY IS HARD SO USING RESIDUE OR TITLE IS COMMON

Gifting real property is hard, which is land, buildings, and fixtures. Helpfully a Will gift of real property using a location does gift all land, buildings, and fixtures there with no need to even describe what's there.

Giving real property using a "legal description" is legally best but it can be very long and hard to do correctly.

This can be lot based, like: "Lots 8 and 9, Block 12, Stewart's addition to Pine Subdivision, an addition to the City of Las Vegas, as recorded in Vol 2 of plats, page 85, Records of Clark County, State of Nevada".

Or it may be an old fashioned description like, "Begin at NE 1/4 of SW 1/4 of Sect. 28, Township 20 S, Range 61 E, M.D.B. & M map line, and then South 50 ft, then East 18 ft, then to point of beginning (a triangle shape).

It is less safe but common to gift real property with plain words, like a house by "I give 21 Ivy Rd., Elko, NV to Leo Ian Lee", or land like "I give all real property in Clark County, NV to Sue Ann Hu". Often both address and legal description are used. It is fine to do a blanket gift, like "I give all real property and fixtures I own to ___".

The legally safest way to gift real property is 1) do nothing specific so it's covered by a Will Residue Clause which covers things not specifically gifted other ways, or 2) have broker or lawyer add names to the land title.

SIMPLE WILL WITH MOST GIFTING DONE BY RESIDUE CLAUSE IS OFTEN BEST

Writing a simple Will without many gifts and much left blank and then using Residue Clause is often best.

If there is a spouse often people do a few small gifts to friends and other family, then use Residue Clause of Will to gift their spouse the Residue, and then name a few fallback persons in the Residue Clause.

If there is no spouse and no child often people do a few small gifts, then gift family or friends the Residue.

A parent with young children if married to other parent often gifts Residue to spouse, and as fallback gifts the Residue to the children. Or if not married a parent mostly gifts to their children using the Residue Clause.

CHAPTER 5
DEBT, MARRIAGE, AND YOUNG CHILD ISSUES

DEBT, MARRIAGE, AND YOUNG CHILD CAN CAUSE ISSUES

This Chapter covers **complex** debt, marriage, and young child issues. Some people can skip some parts.

DEBT ISSUES

PAYING DECEDENT'S DEBTS MAY USE UP RESOURCES

Creditors a decedent owed can ask a judge to be paid from decedent's money and property before some Will gifts and transfers are done. How paying debts occurs is mostly set by law and a Will need not cover this. Paying debts uses some property and money so may affect (in order) the Will Residue, Will general gifts, Will specific gifts, and non-probate transfers. Some things like funeral or probate costs have priority to be paid first. Decedent's spouse or family usually don't have to pay decedent's debts unless they guaranteed or co-signed. People should consider how paying debts may use up money or property, leaving less to carry out Will gifts.

IN NEVADA THE FAMILY HOME OFTEN GOES TO FAMILY

Often a person puts a spouse or minor children on the land title to a house so they get it if the person dies. Often a Will gives family the family home. Or any spouse can do a Country Recorder's "Homestead Declaration" so at a death ownership of a family home goes to a surviving spouse. If no Declaration is done a spouse or children can ask a judge to let them stay for their life or to age 18. Note, Community Property law means a surviving spouse often owns part of a house bought or partly paid for while married, and not giving them the rest can cause awkward shared ownership and legal issues. Helpfully except for creditors with a mortgage, home equity loan, or mechanics liens by law it's hard for creditors to get payment by involving a family house. For many reasons most people give a house to a spouse or if none to minor children by Will or using the title.

BEFORE DEBTS ARE PAID FAMILY CAN CLAIM "FAMILY RIGHTS"

Many states say "family rights" can be claimed by a spouse or minor children before most debts are paid. In Nevada a family can ask for most household items owned by the deceased to go to them (Nevada law N.R.S. 21.090 calls this "exempt property'). Also, a "Family Allowance" taken from the estate can go to a family while probate occurs, which is paid before debts except probate costs, funeral costs, and health care costs of the last illness. Note, due to state law a spouse often has ownership of a half-interest or more in all community property so creditors can find it hard to get payment by involving any of this property. Also in Nevada the "set aside" probate procedure can be used if a decedent left under $100,000 of things and no major real property, and this often lets a spouse or minor children get all of decedent's things without paying debts except costs of probate, funeral costs, and health care costs of decedent's last illness. But if family choose to use these options this uses up money and property so may limit Will gifts and other transfers. Due to all this most people by Will and other ways give mostly to any spouse or minor children.

SECURED DEBTS LIKE MORTGAGE OR VEHICLE LIEN ARE NOT PAID OFF

Secured debts like a house mortgage or vehicle lien on decedent's things are not usually paid off since state law and most Wills say this, mostly to not use up estate resources paying off big debts. A Testator can a) gift in Will money to pay the debt, or b) put in Will an order to pay (like, "I order home mortgage paid off").

MARRIAGE ISSUES

"COMMUNITY PROPERTY" LAW APPLIES TO SPOUSES IN NEVADA

Nine states mostly in U.S. West for married people use "Community Property" law, like <u>Nevada</u>, Texas, and California. Other states use "Separate Property" law. Things can be complex if people recently moved. A few people sign a contract about Community Property usually before a wedding. **The law is complex**.

MARRIED SPOUSES MAY OWN MOST THINGS 50/50 EVEN WAGES AND SALARY

Community Property law says <u>residents if married share 50/50 and have a half-interest in money and property either spouse gets which is related in any major way to physical or mental effort while married</u>. Shared things are called "community property" and all else is called "separate property". This law is from Spanish and other traditions, seeing marriage like a partnership, and so if a person's spouse dies the person has something to live on. Many states have laws to give any spouse a lot so they have resources to live on. <u>So, wages, salary, and income related to labor are usually community property no matter what spouses say</u>.

SHOWING THINGS ARE NOT COMMUNITY PROPERTY CAN BE HARD

A judge will accept what people say is Community Property, but if anyone disputes this the law presumes a married person's things are community property till proven otherwise. Good records, separate accounts, or discussing ownership with witnesses can help **but is rarely done**. Putting 1 name on an account or title to a thing doesn't change its nature. <u>Many couples end up with **most** property and money as community property</u>. Examples of separate property are an inheritance or gift given to 1 spouse, personal injury lawsuit money, engagement and wedding rings, and anything owned before marriage including savings and any property. Separate property can come from tracing to other separate property, like if pre-marriage money pays half a car's price then it is half separate, or if pre-marital property is sold for cash it is all separate. But using physical or mental effort while married on separate property can make it be partly community property, like doing big repairs or remodeling, actively managing a business, or actively trading a collection or stocks.

MARRIED PEOPLE FACE ISSUES AND HAVE SOME OPTIONS WHEN GIFTING

Married people face some issues with gifting by Will and other ways things, including as this book has said due to community property, family rights, and other issues. Married people have some options.

First, to avoid issues many people just give everything wholly to their spouse by Will or other ways.

Second, some people are careful to only gift separate property to persons not their spouse by Will and other ways, and then have all community property go to a spouse. But this can be hard to do with certainty.

Third, many people trust <u>if they give most money and property to the spouse and family (like over 90% and the family home) then a spouse won't object to a small bit of community property a decedent gave to others</u>, and instead will cooperate in carrying out the Will. A spouse often doesn't want the hassle, to seem selfish, or risk a lawsuit just to keep a half-interest in a little bit of community property a decedent gave to someone.

YOUNG CHILD ISSUES

"GUARDIAN OF THE PERSON" GIVES PERSONAL CARE TO CHILD

If a parent dies with a child under 18 the other natural or adopted parent (but not step-parent) usually gets control of a child including health care, school, and home issues, unless the parent is proven unfit in court which is rare. But in case it is needed (like if both parents are dead) Wills often name a "Guardian of the Person" to give this personal care to a child, often naming a healthy and willing family member or friend.

"GUARDIAN OF THE ESTATE" MANAGES A CHILD'S MONEY AND PROPERTY

Since a child until 18 can't easily manage money or property many Wills name a "Guardian of the Estate" to help. They will manage a child's property and money, decide how to use these for a child's costs like living costs, school, and health care, and usually at 18 all goes to the child. People paying for needed things can ask to be paid from a child's funds. Judges often hold a yearly hearing to review any spending. Note, most Wills at their end also say Executor may let a "Custodian" they pick manage a minor's property and money, spend it for the minor's benefit, and often when minor is usually 18 give them anything left. This is allowed by the new helpful "Uniform Transfers To Minors Act" law to let a Custodian mostly do what a Guardian of the Estate does but avoids most costs, work, and court hearings.

THIS BOOK'S WILLS NAME THE SAME PERSON AS BOTH KINDS OF GUARDIAN

This book's Will forms have a spot to name a person to be Guardian of the Person and, also, Guardian of the Estate. Not bothering to name different people is common since parents dying is rare, usually a child gets things only if both parents are dead so a Guardian of the Person will be involved, people chosen as wise enough to raise children often are at least OK with money, and a Guardian of the Person if they disagree with spending may argue or sue. People can modify a Will to name different people for these 2 jobs if they want.

A PERSON TO BE A GUARDIAN MUST BE AT LEAST AGE 18

To be a Guardian a person must be at least 18. The preference of the last living parent usually controls. After age 14 a child can say who they'd prefer for a judge to consider. A Guardian needn't be a U.S. citizen or state resident but being local makes work easier, and they may need to name a local person to get mail. Usually no one with a criminal record involving a felony or child may be a Guardian, and a judge may block or remove people who are unsuitable. If no Will names someone or they're unavailable a judge can pick someone but this may cause family arguments. Naming 2 people to be Guardian <u>at the same time</u> is rare since this may problems and since any 1 person named is trusted, but some people name a married couple. Some Wills name a 2nd person <u>in case the first person is unavailable</u> to serve if needed, but most people skip this since it is rarely needed, if seen a Will can be re-done, or a judge can act. If wanted words can be added to a Will to add a second person, like "or if they are reasonably unable to serve I name ___ to serve".

PICKING GUARDIANS RARELY MATTERS DESPITE PARENTS WORRYING

A young child having parents die is rare so parents shouldn't worry that much about this. A very large U.S. study of 311,900 people found 72,240 were under 18 and of these 2014 had lost 1 parent (2.78%) and just 97 both parents (just 0.13%), so losing parents is very rare. *Census Life Factors Mortality Study #288*.

CHAPTER 6
BASIC IDEAS ABOUT HEALTH CARE FORMS

SOME BASIC IDEAS HELP PEOPLE UNDERSTAND HEALTH CARE FORMS

Some ideas help people understand health care forms.

■ By law people control their own health care unless "incapacitated" by inability to a) be conscious enough, b) be rational enough, or c) communicate verbally or by written notes. Unless incapacitated people just tell doctors what health care they want and legal documents don't matter. In actuality most people keep control of health care till death or until no big options remain, but people worry they may be incapacitated a long time.

■ Parents do have power over health care of their children under age 18.

■ If an adult 18 or older becomes incapacitated the adult's closest family like spouse or adult child can make emergency decisions but they usually must then rush to a judge to get more power if no form gives them power over health care.

■ In forms a person can be named to have control of health care if needed, who is often called "Agent".

■ In forms people can give written health care instructions doctors, family, Agent, and others must obey.

■ **Young people** are less often ill so often skip health care forms. Some **married people** do a form to give a spouse power over health care if they are incapacitated. Some **young adults** give this power to parents.

■ Pain relief like pain drugs and "comfort care" is usually given even if forms say to stop or limit other care.

■ Most people do 1 fairly long health care form with spots for instructions and to name an Agent in case they are incapacitated. Names for this form varies. Other forms are mostly only done by oldest or sickest people.

■ For rare cases stopping health care ("pulling plug") likely will matter due to type of illness or extreme age:

-- most people do nothing special and trust family or Agent to decide on stopping care based on changing complex factors like pain, cost, hassle, suffering and time of treatment, beliefs, and chances of recovery;

-- a few people do a serious document to say to stop most health care if **later** doctors decide a person a) is incapacitated, b) has irrevocable terminal condition or likely won't regain good consciousness, and c) further medical care won't help (this action is often called a "Living Will" though names of forms vary);

-- a few people do a serious document to **starting immediately** block health care listed, often called a "Do-Not-Resuscitate" if just about "resuscitation" or called a "Physician's Order" if about many treatments.

■ This book has 3 legal forms about health care which are all fairly standard, which are: 1) Durable Power Of Attorney For Health Care Decisions, 2) Living Will Declaration, and 3) Do-Not-Resuscitate legal forms.

CHAPTER 7
FORM 1: LAST WILL AND TESTAMENT (STANDARD)

FORM 1 IS A STANDARD WILL THAT IS FLEXIBLE AND WITHOUT GUARDIAN

Form 1 is a standard Will that is flexible and lets a person control some things after their death. This form has no part about a Guardian so this form is for a person with no minor child under age 18.

FORM IS WILL WITH SEVERAL PARTS

This form at start has place for person doing Will (Testator) to write full legal name (unless they dislike it and rarely used it), and write county they currently reside in (a Will is still valid if people move later).

The 1st paragraph, "Gifts", has many spaces to make either specific gifts of particular property or general gifts like of money. People can delete, copy and paste to add more, or leave blank these gift lines.

The 2nd paragraph, "Separate Writings", says to follow any separate writings done apart from the Will that gifts tangible personal property in way allowed by law.

The 3rd paragraph, "Residue", has a Residue Clause to say any property and money left after other Will parts and any other transfers is gifted to persons as the Residue Clause directs.

The 4th paragraph, "Administration", has space to name a "Personal Representative" to do things after the Testator's death (this newer term in Nevada is mostly replacing the older term of "Executor" for this).

The 5th paragraph, "Miscellaneous", has paragraphs of legal language to help avoid certain legal issues.

Last is paragraph for person doing Will to sign, and paragraph for 2 witnesses to sign and put addresses.

WILL'S RESIDUE CLAUSE HAS 2 PLACES TO NAME PERSONS TO GET THINGS

In a Will "Residue Clause" any property and money of Testator left after all Will gifts and other transfers is distributed as the clause directs. Many people use a Residue Clause to gift most things to not have to describe every single thing and for other legal reasons. In this Will form's Residue Clause there is:

1) a 1st space to name 1 or more persons to get the Residue, and if any named here have not survived and died before the Will maker then any other persons named here take their share,

2) a 2nd space to name people to get things if all in 1st space died before Will maker, and if any people named here didn't survive their shares go to "lineal descendants" like their children.

Most people name in 1st space a spouse or closest family or closest friends, and in 2nd space next closest family or friends. This may seem complex but usually people in the 1st area of the Clause will get things.

TESTATOR AND 2 WITNESSES WHILE TOGETHER SIGN WILL

This Will form after being filled out (except bits intentionally left blank) to be valid must be signed by person doing the Will (called Testator) in front of 2 witnesses at least age 18 who then also sign the Will. Testator and witnesses should be in 1 room and see each person sign. Witnesses usually just read the 1 paragraph they sign. Usually the witnesses are not themselves named in any Will gifts and also usually not named to be Executor, Guardian, or similar in the Will. The Testator need not initial the Will pages. Testator and witnesses showing each other ID is common. Though not required often Testator says a thing like, "My name is _____ and this is my Will that I do voluntarily and want you 2 people to witness". Once done a Will should be kept where it can be gotten quickly after a death like in a desk, files, or a safe.

LAST WILL AND TESTAMENT

I, _____, of _____ County, Nevada, do revoke all prior Wills, Testaments, and Codicils, and do make, publish, and declare this as my Will. I am of sound mind and under no duress or undue influence and acting voluntarily.

1. GIFTS. I give these gifts in this Will, but to get a gift in this section the recipient must survive me except as otherwise stated below.

I give _____ to _____.

I give _____ to _____.

I give _____ to _____.

I give _____ to _____.

I give _____ to _____.

I give _____ to _____.

I give _____ to _____.

I give _____ to _____.

2. SEPARATE WRITINGS. I may do writings separate from this Will to gift tangible personal property as allowed by state law including Nevada Revised Statutes 133.045 and such writings should be followed. This Will does not revoke any such writings that exist. A gift in such a writing to a person who does not survive me is canceled and has no effect. Any such writing not found within 90 days of my death is canceled and has no effect.

3. RESIDUE. I give the residue, rest, and remainder of my estate, my money and property of any kind and nature, and anything I have an interest in so long as it was not transferred by other Will provisions (all of which is called the "residue"), as follows:

   a) to _____ who survive me with persons just named who survive me taking the share of non-survivors, then

   b) to _____ and if any of the persons just named do not survive me their part goes to their lineal descendants per stirpes.

4. ADMINISTRATION. I name and appoint _____ as Personal Representative including for me, my Will, and my estate.

5. MISCELLANEOUS. The following applies to this Will and generally.

Nevada is my primary residence and its laws should apply to this Will.

Priority of Will gifts of the same type is based on the order they are written.

In this document no unfilled part is a mistake and residue spaces may be left blank.

The words "give" and "gift" also means a devise, bequest, grant, legacy, or similar.

A gift of property no longer owned by Testator at death shall lapse and be of no effect including no payment of money shall be done in its place, all without ademption.

If a gift or section reasonably mentions survival in any way then survival is an absolute condition and anti-lapse laws or similar have no effect.

Unless a Will gift specifies otherwise if a Will gift goes to multiple recipients if any do not survive Testator their part to them lapses and instead goes to other surviving recipients.

Any failure to make more or any Will gifts to current children or current spouse at the time I do this Will is intentional and not a mistake to remedy.

No gift or transfer I made during my life to a person reduces or offsets a Will gift unless during my life I expressly usually called it a "loan" or "advancement".

Unless another meaning is clearly shown by context use of plural includes the singular and vice versa, and also masculine, feminine, and neuter words are used interchangeably. Unless another meaning is shown "they" means both one person and multiple persons.

Unless a Will says otherwise a secured debt like mortgage or lien shall not be paid off, recipient of a Will gift of property takes it subject to any debts, and no such recipient who later loses the property to a debtor or who pays a debtor to avoid foreclosure or other loss may require the estate, heirs, devisees, or others to pay recipient back or do anything.

I request and authorize any informal, summary, and quick probate or similar action. Any Personal Representative may act independently with no supervision of any court, including independent administration, and without doing any action or filings in court.

I give any Personal Representative a) the fullest authority, powers, and discretion allowed by state law, b) authority to lease, sell, mortgage, convey, or retain property including real property in any such manner and time they deem helpful or proper, and c) authority to settle or pay claims or debts at any time they in their sole discretion choose. Any Personal Representative shall also have all powers found in Nevada Revised Statutes existing on the date of this Will and any other powers hereafter conferred by law.

A Personal Representative shall have sole discretion how to balance people's feelings and pick property or divide a gift to carry out a general gift or a gift to multiple persons.

If context permits the terms Personal Representative, Executor, and Administrator are interchangeable as if all were written, and Conservator is interchangeable with Guardian of the Estate and Guardian of Property. The term Residue also means Residuary.

I request any lawyers be paid hourly or as agreed and not by percentage fee schedule.

The residue includes lapsed or failed gifts, insurance paid to estate, inheritances owed me, and property I had or have a power of appointment or testamentary disposition over.

Any Personal Representative, Executor, Administrator, Guardian of any type, Conservator, Custodian, and any fiduciary under this Will or otherwise shall qualify and serve without bond, security, surety, or any similar thing.

If part of this Will is by law invalid or unenforceable other provisions remain in effect.

Any Personal Representative in their sole discretion may at any time transfer money or property of a minor under age 18 to a Custodian under Nevada's Uniform Act on Transfers to Minors law or any similar law anywhere. The Custodian holding money and property can make discretionary payments of any kind and to any recipient to benefit the minor, and later pay any remainder to a minor at age 18. When doing this no bond, court action, or anything is required. Any Personal Representative may select the Custodian including themselves but if they do not I name for this the Guardian of the Estate named in this Will.

TESTATOR

I, as Testator of this Will, do now declare, publish, and sign this instrument as my Will this __ day of _____, 20___.

_____
Testator signature

DECLARATION OF WITNESSES

Under penalty of perjury pursuant to the law of the State of Nevada, the undersigned, _____ and _____, declare that the following is true of their own knowledge: That they witnessed the execution of the foregoing Will of the Testator, _____; that the Testator subscribed the Will and declared it to be his or her last Will and testament in their presence; that they thereafter subscribed the Will as witnesses in the presence of the Testator and in the presence of each other and at the request of the Testator; and that the Testator at the time of the execution of the Will appeared to them to be of full age and of sound mind and memory.

Dated this ___ day of _____, 20____.

_____   _____
Declarant   Address

_____   _____
Declarant   Address

CHAPTER 8
FORM 2: LAST WILL AND TESTAMENT (GUARDIAN)

FORM 2 IS BASIC WILL WITH GUARDIAN CLAUSE FOR YOUNG CHILD

Form 2 is a Will with a Guardian part to be used by a person with a minor child under age 18.

FORM IS WILL WITH SEVERAL PARTS

This form at start has place for person doing Will (Testator) to write full legal name (unless they dislike it and rarely used it), and write county they currently reside in (a Will is still valid if people move later).

The 1st paragraph, "Gifts", has many spaces to make either specific gifts of particular property or general gifts like of money. People can delete, copy and paste to add more, or leave blank these gift lines.

The 2nd paragraph, "Separate Writings", says to follow any separate writings done apart from the Will that gifts tangible personal property in way allowed by law.

The 3rd paragraph, "Residue", has a Residue Clause to say any property and money left after other Will parts and any other transfers is gifted to persons as the Residue Clause directs.

The 4th paragraph, "Administration", has space to name a "Personal Representative" to do things after the Testator's death (this newer term in Nevada is mostly replacing the older term of "Executor" for this).

The 5th paragraph, "Guardian", lets the person name a Guardian of the Person to if needed care for a young child (if no parent is available), and a Guardian of the Estate to manage a child's property and money.

The 6th paragraph, "Miscellaneous", has paragraphs of legal language to help avoid certain legal issues.

Last is paragraph for person doing Will to sign, and paragraph for 2 witnesses to sign and put addresses.

WILL'S RESIDUE CLAUSE HAS 2 PLACES TO NAME PERSONS TO GET THINGS

In a Will "Residue Clause" any property and money of Testator left after all Will gifts and other transfers is distributed as the clause directs. Many people use a Residue Clause to gift most things to not have to describe every single thing and for other legal reasons. In this Will form's Residue Clause there is:

1) a 1st space to name 1 or more persons to get the Residue, and if any named here have not survived and died before the Will maker then any other persons named here take their share,

2) a 2nd space to name people to get things if all in 1st space died before Will maker, and if any people named here didn't survive their shares go to "lineal descendants" like their children.

Most people name in 1st space a spouse or closest family or closest friends, and in 2nd space next closest family or friends. This may seem complex but usually people in the 1st area of the Clause will get things.

TESTATOR AND 2 WITNESSES WHILE TOGETHER SIGN WILL

This Will form after being filled out (except bits intentionally left blank) to be valid must be signed by person doing the Will (called Testator) in front of 2 witnesses at least age 18 who then also sign the Will. Testator and witnesses should be in 1 room and see each person sign. Witnesses usually just read the 1 paragraph they sign. Usually witnesses are not themselves named in any Will gifts and also usually not named to be Executor, Guardian, or similar in the Will. The Testator need not initial the Will pages. Testator and witnesses showing each other ID is common. Though not required often Testator says a thing like, "My name is _____ and this is my Will that I do voluntarily and want you 2 people to witness".

LAST WILL AND TESTAMENT

I, _____, of _____ County, Nevada, do revoke all prior Wills, Testaments, and Codicils, and do make, publish, and declare this as my Will. I am of sound mind and under no duress or undue influence and acting voluntarily.

1. GIFTS. I give these gifts in this Will, but to get a gift in this section the recipient must survive me except as otherwise stated below.

I give _____ to _____.

I give _____ to _____.

I give _____ to _____.

I give _____ to _____.

I give _____ to _____.

I give _____ to _____.

I give _____ to _____.

I give _____ to _____.

2. SEPARATE WRITINGS. I may do writings separate from this Will to gift tangible personal property as allowed by state law including Nevada Revised Statutes 133.045 and such writings should be followed. This Will does not revoke any such writings that exist. A gift in such a writing to a person who does not survive me is canceled and has no effect. Any such writing not found within 90 days of my death is canceled and has no effect.

3. RESIDUE. I give the residue, rest, and remainder of my estate, my money and property of any kind and nature, and anything I have an interest in so long as it was not transferred by other Will provisions (all of which is called the "residue"), as follows:

a) to _____ who survive me with persons just named who survive me taking the share of non-survivors, then

b) to _____ and if any of the persons just named do not survive me their part goes to their lineal descendants per stirpes.

4. ADMINISTRATION. I name and appoint _____ as Personal Representative including for me, my Will, and my estate.

5. GUARDIAN. I name to serve when proper _____ as Guardian of the Person with control, authority, and custody of any minor child, and also as Guardian of the Estate with control and authority over any minor child's property, money, and estate

6. MISCELLANEOUS. The following applies to this Will and generally.

Nevada is my primary residence and its laws should apply to this Will.

Priority of Will gifts of the same type is based on the order they are written.

In this document no unfilled part is a mistake and residue spaces may be left blank.

The words "give" and "gift" also means a devise, bequest, grant, legacy, or similar.

A gift of property no longer owned by Testator at death shall lapse and be of no effect including no payment of money shall be done in its place, all without ademption.

If a gift or section reasonably mentions survival in any way then survival is an absolute condition and anti-lapse laws or similar have no effect.

Unless a Will gift specifies otherwise if a Will gift goes to multiple recipients if any do not survive Testator their part to them lapses and instead goes to other surviving recipients.

Any failure to make more or any Will gifts to current children or current spouse at the time I do this Will is intentional and not a mistake to remedy.

No gift or transfer I made during my life to a person reduces or offsets a Will gift unless during my life I expressly usually called it a "loan" or "advancement".

Unless another meaning is clearly shown by context use of plural includes the singular and vice versa, and also masculine, feminine, and neuter words are used interchangeably. Unless another meaning is shown "they" means both one person and multiple persons.

Unless a Will says otherwise a secured debt like mortgage or lien shall not be paid off, recipient of a Will gift of property takes it subject to any debts, and no such recipient who later loses the property to a debtor or who pays a debtor to avoid foreclosure or other loss may require the estate, heirs, devisees, or others to pay recipient back or do anything.

I request and authorize any informal, summary, and quick probate or similar action. Any Personal Representative may act independently with no supervision of any court, including independent administration, and without doing any action or filings in court.

I give any Personal Representative a) the fullest authority, powers, and discretion allowed by state law, b) authority to lease, sell, mortgage, convey, or retain property including real property in any such manner and time they deem helpful or proper, and c) authority to settle or pay claims or debts at any time they in their sole discretion choose. Any Personal Representative shall also have all powers found in Nevada Revised Statutes existing on the date of this Will and any other powers hereafter conferred by law.

A Personal Representative shall have sole discretion how to balance people's feelings and pick property or divide a gift to carry out a general gift or a gift to multiple persons.

If context permits the terms Personal Representative, Executor, and Administrator are interchangeable as if all were written, and Conservator is interchangeable with Guardian

of the Estate and Guardian of Property. The term Residue also means Residuary.

I request any lawyers be paid hourly or as agreed and not by percentage fee schedule.

The residue includes lapsed or failed gifts, insurance paid to estate, inheritances owed me, and property I had or have a power of appointment or testamentary disposition over.

Any Personal Representative, Executor, Administrator, Guardian of any type, Conservator, Custodian, and any fiduciary under this Will or otherwise shall qualify and serve without bond, security, surety, or any similar thing.

If part of this Will is by law invalid or unenforceable other provisions remain in effect.

Any Personal Representative in their sole discretion may at any time transfer money or property of a minor under age 18 to a Custodian under Nevada's Uniform Act on Transfers to Minors law or any similar law anywhere. The Custodian holding money and property can make discretionary payments of any kind and to any recipient to benefit the minor, and later pay any remainder to a minor at age 18. When doing this no bond, court action, or anything is required. Any Personal Representative may select the Custodian including themselves but if they do not I name for this the Guardian of the Estate named in this Will.

TESTATOR

I, as Testator of this Will, do now declare, publish, and sign this instrument as my Will this __ day of _____, 20___.

_____
Testator signature

DECLARATION OF WITNESSES

Under penalty of perjury pursuant to the law of the State of Nevada, the undersigned, _____ and _____, declare that the following is true of their own knowledge: That they witnessed the execution of the foregoing Will of the Testator, _____; that the Testator subscribed the Will and declared it to be his or her last Will and testament in their presence; that they thereafter subscribed the Will as witnesses in the presence of the Testator and in the presence of each other and at the request of the Testator; and that the Testator at the time of the execution of the Will appeared to them to be of full age and of sound mind and memory.

Dated this ___ day of _____, 20___.

_____   _____
Declarant   Address

_____   _____
Declarant   Address

CHAPTER 9
FORM 3: HANDWRITTEN WILL

WILL CAN SKIP USING THE NORMAL 2 WITNESSES IF IT IS ALL HANDWRITTEN

A "Handwritten Will" (often called a "Holographic Will" by lawyers) is a Will that is easier to do by not needing the usual 2 witnesses see it signed if it is completely handwritten by the person doing the Will.

HANDWRITTEN WILL WITHOUT WITNESSES IS ALLOWED IN NEVADA

In 27 states including Nevada a person doing a Will can skip having the usual 2 witnesses for a Will if: 1) it is all handwritten by Testator doing Will (not photocopied, typed, computer printed, or handwritten by anyone else), and 2) it is signed and dated. Many people call this a "Handwritten Will", and lawyers call this a "Holographic Will" (Holo means Whole and Graph means Image in the Greek language lawyers often use). State legislators allow this since handwriting is hard to forge, people may be in emergency or rush, witnesses may be scarce in the countryside or emergencies, it is private, it can be cheap by skipping complexity and people, and it is traditional especially in rural places. States that allow Handwritten Wills have about 55% of the U.S. population so Handwritten Wills are common, and in these states these are about 5% of all Wills. Lawmakers want people to have this simple option. See states with Handwritten Wills on map below in dark.

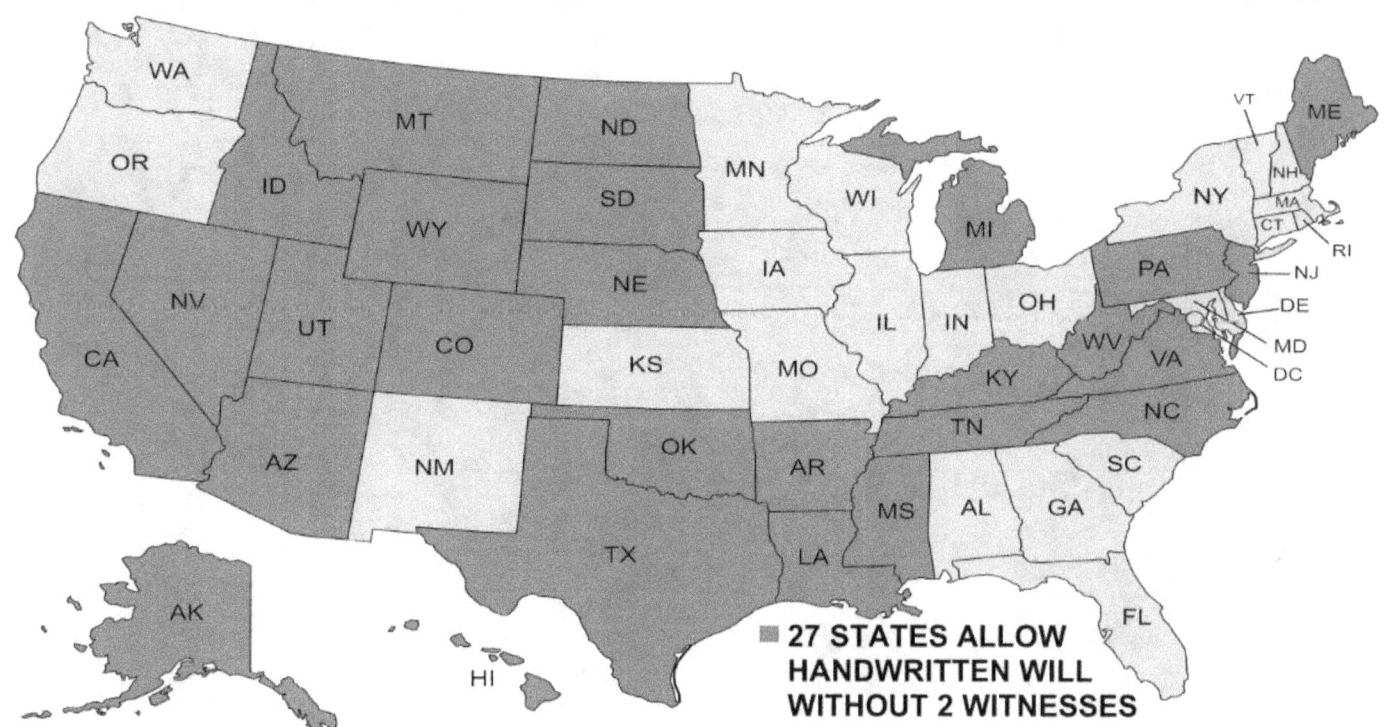

27 STATES ALLOW HANDWRITTEN WILL WITHOUT 2 WITNESSES

HANDWRITTEN WILLS ARE USUALLY FINE BUT REQUIRE LATER WORK

Some lawyers warn against Handwritten Wills saying they often read confusingly, skip legal words that help in some cases, and are found invalid more often – but some studies show they are liked and usually fine. After a death to use a Handwritten Will in court a family member, friend, or handwriting expert must sign an affidavit or say in court the Will looks like Testator's handwriting, which can be a hassle. But a normal Will with 2 witnesses if no Self-Proving Affidavit or Declaration was done also may require some work to use it. Handwritten Wills are more often used by people who are young, in a hurry, who want to fix a mistake, about to go on a trip and want to name a Guardian, who moved to a new state, or who plan a better Will later.

WORDS ON BOTTOM OF PAGE CAN BE USED FOR A HANDWRITTEN WILL

People can do a Handwritten Will in a sentence that is legal but may leave out helpful parts, for example:

"As my Will I give my estate and all else I have to Judy Smith who shall be Personal Representative."

But it is recommended people use more complex words for Handwritten Will shown on bottom of this page.

To do this people should change the names and words below on this page to match what they want done.

These words below mostly say they gift things to persons whose names are written in who survive (live past) the person doing the Will. If all named people are dead then state "intestate law" usually controls and gives things to nearest other family, but laws are complex and it may be best to re-do a Will to name new people.

The last paragraph about Guardians for children can be skipped if a person has no child under age 18.

The Will must be all handwritten and signed by person doing it on some paper, and using pencil is fine.

WILL

1. My name is David Paul Hud and I now live in Clark County, Nevada. I revoke any prior Wills and Codicils and declare this to be my Will.

2. I give my estate and all else I have to Ann Eve Hud and Luke John Hud who survive me.

3. I name Ann Eve Hud as Personal Representative for me, my Will, and my estate, and no bond or surerty shall be required of them. I request informal probate.

4. For any child of mine I name Mary Sue Hill as Guardian of the Person and as Guardian of the Estate for their estate and property.

May 8, 2022   David Paul Hud

CHAPTER 10
FORM 4: SELF-PROVING AFFIDAVIT

FORM CAN BE DONE WITH WILL TO SOMETIMES AVOID LATER LEGAL WORK

This form can help with later legal work involved with using a Will after a death. This form must be completed in front of a person who is a notary. This Self-Proving Affidavit form is a statutory form found in Nevada state law for people to use if wanted.

HELPS LATER SHOW WILL WAS PROPERLY SIGNED BUT IS OFTEN SKIPPED

The Self-Proving Affidavit when trying to use a Will after a death can help prove it was properly signed. Without this more work may be needed later, like later a witness must say in court or do a writing describing how a Will was signed (or other proof). If this form is not done there is more risk a Will is not followed later. But Nevada law does say if the paragraph the witnesses sign in a Will has certain words about "perjury" then this is a "Declaration" that usually avoids later need for more proof even if no notary sees people sign. The law at Nevada Revised Statutes 133.050 shows the exact words needed for this, and all this book's Will forms use these words for witnesses to sign. Only 5 states have such helpful laws like Nevada that do this. Overall, of people doing Wills about half skip doing a Self-Proving Affidavit mostly due to Nevada law, due to the hassle of finding a notary each time a Will is done, and since it mostly just saves later minor work for people who are probably happy to do a bit of work to get things using a Will. Most attorneys do recommend using a Self-Proving Affidavit form but this is not required to have a valid Will.

FORM IS DONE BY TESTATOR AND 2 WITNESSES SIGNING WITH A NOTARY

To complete the Self-Proving Affidavit form a person who is a notary (also called "notary public") must see form signed by Testator and the 2 witnesses to the Will signing, and then the notary notarizes the form. The form is often done within minutes of when a Will is signed but it also can be done anytime later (even months later) when Testator and 2 witnesses can meet a notary. Once done the Self-Proving Affidavit is often kept with the Will it supports.

SELF–PROVING AFFIDAVIT

State of Nevada   }
                 }ss.

County of _____ }

(Date) _____

   Then and there personally appeared _____ and _____,
who, being duly sworn, depose and say: That they witnessed the execution of the
foregoing will of the Testator, _____; that the Testator subscribed
the will and declared it to be his or her last Will and testament in their presence; that they
thereafter subscribed the Will as witnesses in the presence of the Testator and in the
presence of each other and at the request of the Testator; and that the Testator at the time
of the execution of the Will appeared to them to be of full age and of sound mind and
memory.

                _____
                Affiant

                _____
                Affiant

Subscribed and sworn to before me this
_____ day of the month of _____ of the year _____.

_____
Notary Public

CHAPTER 11
FORM 5: TANGIBLE PERSONAL PROPERTY LIST

LETS GIFTS OF SOME PROPERTY BE EASILY MADE OUTSIDE A WILL

This form lets people before or after a Will is done easily add some gifts of property they want to occur after their death. This form is sometimes called a "Memorandum", a "Gift List", or often just a "List".

FORM GIVES EASY QUICK WAY TO WRITE MORE GIFTS

The form in this Chapter, often just called a List form, lets a person before or after their Will has been done easily write more gifts of property to occur after their death without the hassle of doing a new Will. The law says for a List to be used a Will must say they can be used, and all this book's Will forms say this. If a List and a Will gift the same item then by law the Will is followed. People can do many List pages over time and all can count. If multiple Lists gift the same item the more recent List controls. People can change Lists by crossing out, erasing, or adding words, but then should put a new date and signature at the bottom. To cut delay this book's forms say a List not found by someone within 90 days of a death will be ignored.

It may help understanding to show the Nevada law allowing Lists, NRS 133.045, which says:

Disposition of certain tangible personal property by reference to list or statement; requirements.

1. [A] will may refer to a written statement or list, including, without limitation, a written statement or list contained in an electronic record, to dispose of items of tangible personal property not otherwise specifically disposed of by the will, other than money, evidences of indebtedness, documents of title, securities and property used in a trade or business.
2. To be admissible as evidence of the intended disposition, the statement or list must contain:
    (a) The date of its execution.
    (b) A title indicating its purpose.
    (c) A reference to the will to which it relates.
    (d) A reasonably certain description of the items to be disposed of and the names of the devisees.
    (e) The testator's handwritten signature [...]
3. The statement or list may be:
    (a) Referred to as a writing to be in existence at the time of the testator's death.
    (b) Prepared before or after the execution of the will.
    (c) Altered by the testator after its preparation[...]

FORM CAN ONLY GIFT "TANGIBLE PERSONAL PROPERTY"

By law a List form can only gift "tangible personal property", so only tangible (touchable) things and not most accounts or investments where ownership is tied to papers or some entity like a corporation or trust. It also can't gift "real property" (land or buildings). It also can't gift money even the coin or paper money are antiques. Though not required most people do not put in a List property used in a trade or business or also mobile homes. Most people use a List to gift furniture, clothes, cars, boats, jewelry, electronics, antiques, household tools, art, and similar items. Improper property written in a form is ignored.

TO COMPLETE GIFT LIST A PERSON JUST SIGNS AND DATES IT

A List form just must be signed and dated by person who is doing it. Once completed any List form pages are often kept with a Will. To cancel a List it can be thrown away or destroyed or just crossed out.

TANGIBLE PERSONAL PROPERTY LIST

This writing is referred to in my Will and gives tangible personal property at my death as allowed by state law including by Nevada Revised Statutes 133.045. I may do multiple pages like this which all should be followed with the more recent controlling any conflicts. Any page not found within 90 days of my death is canceled. If a person getting a gift below does not survive me that gift to them is canceled.

PROPERTY ITEMS		NAMES OF RECIPIENTS
_____	to	_____
_____	to	_____
_____	to	_____
_____	to	_____
_____	to	_____
_____	to	_____
_____	to	_____
_____	to	_____
_____	to	_____
_____	to	_____
_____	to	_____
_____	to	_____
_____	to	_____
_____	to	_____
_____	to	_____
_____	to	_____
_____	to	_____

DATE:_____   SIGNED:_____

CHAPTER 12
FORM 6: DURABLE POWER OF ATTORNEY FOR HEALTH CARE DECISIONS

FORM LETS PERSON NAME HEALTH CARE AGENT AND GIVE INSTRUCTIONS

This statutory form lets people name an Agent and give instructions to control health care if later needed.

FORM CAN NAME "AGENT" FOR HEALTH CARE AND GIVE INSTRUCTIONS

The form lets someone be named as "Health Care Agent" to control health care if later the person doing the form is incapacitated. This person is often called "Attorney-in-Fact' or just "Agent". Often named Agent is a spouse, adult child, relative, or friend. Naming a family member as Agent can avoid need to rush to see a judge for more power. Workers at a place giving health care usually shouldn't be Agent unless they are a family relative. Additional "alternate" persons can be named to act if others don't, but this is rarely needed. The form has areas for general instructions and picking options, but many people skip saying much since they trust their Agent and if any health care instructions aren't clear this can cause delay or legal problems. There is an area to say wishes about living arrangements, but many people skip this and trust their family. There is an area on stopping life-sustaining treatment (the "Statement of Desires Concerning Treatment" area). Many people skip this and just trust their Agent or family, or do a separate "Living Will" form. But some people use this area, and initial boxes to pick from some options and then maybe handwrite orders to stop care, like:

"If I am no longer able to make decisions about my medical treatment and my attending physicians think I have an incurable and irreversible condition that without life-sustaining treatment will kill me in a relatively short time (a terminal condition), then I direct my attending physicians to a) keep me comfortable, b) allow natural death to occur, c) do not give life-sustaining treatment or other medical interventions to try to extend my life, and d) do not give nutrition and fluids by tube or other medical means".

PERSON SIGNS FORM IN FRONT OF EITHER NOTARY OR 2 WITNESSES

The form must be signed in front of either a person who is a notary who then notarizes the form, or 2 witnesses who then sign. A person doing the form can't use as a witness someone in any way involved in giving them health care, and also at least 1 of the witnesses my sign a second area to say they are not related to the person doing the form or entitled like by Will to any part of their estate, money, or property. Once done this form usually is shown to all places that may give care to put in the person's medical file to be followed. To cancel the form a person should tell Agent and usually also tell all places shown the form. Note, to use this form if a person is so sick they're in a hospital, facility for groups or skilled nursing, or home for residential care a doctor may need to a "Certificate Of Competency To Executor Power Of Attorney".

CAN FILE FORM IN "NEVADA LOCKBOX" AT SECRETARY OF STATE'S OFFICE

A person can file this form at the "Nevada Lockbox" filing system run by the Nevada Secretary of State. See **www.nvsos.gov**. This lets people file forms so hospitals and others can look up if a person has done these. After filing people will be mailed a "Lockbox wallet card" to help show a form was done and that it is filed, or people can make and carry a handmade wallet card (see this end of this Chapter). Most people do skip the Lockbox and just make sure hospitals and other places are directly shown any health care forms.

DURABLE POWER OF ATTORNEY FOR HEALTH CARE DECISIONS

(Nevada Revised Statutes 162A.860)

WARNING TO PERSON EXECUTING THIS DOCUMENT

THIS IS AN IMPORTANT LEGAL DOCUMENT. IT CREATES A DURABLE POWER OF ATTORNEY FOR HEALTH CARE. BEFORE EXECUTING THIS DOCUMENT, YOU SHOULD KNOW THESE IMPORTANT FACTS:

1. THIS DOCUMENT GIVES THE PERSON YOU DESIGNATE AS YOUR AGENT THE POWER TO MAKE HEALTH CARE DECISIONS FOR YOU. THIS POWER IS SUBJECT TO ANY LIMITATIONS OR STATEMENT OF YOUR DESIRES THAT YOU INCLUDE IN THIS DOCUMENT. THE POWER TO MAKE HEALTH CARE DECISIONS FOR YOU MAY INCLUDE CONSENT, REFUSAL OF CONSENT OR WITHDRAWAL OF CONSENT TO ANY CARE, TREATMENT, SERVICE OR PROCEDURE TO MAINTAIN, DIAGNOSE OR TREAT A PHYSICAL OR MENTAL CONDITION. YOU MAY STATE IN THIS DOCUMENT ANY TYPES OF TREATMENT OR PLACEMENTS THAT YOU DO NOT DESIRE.

2. THE PERSON YOU DESIGNATE IN THIS DOCUMENT HAS A DUTY TO ACT CONSISTENT WITH YOUR DESIRES AS STATED IN THIS DOCUMENT OR OTHERWISE MADE KNOWN OR, IF YOUR DESIRES ARE UNKNOWN, TO ACT IN YOUR BEST INTERESTS.

3. EXCEPT AS YOU OTHERWISE SPECIFY IN THIS DOCUMENT, THE POWER OF THE PERSON YOU DESIGNATE TO MAKE HEALTH CARE DECISIONS FOR YOU MAY INCLUDE THE POWER TO CONSENT TO YOUR DOCTOR OR ADVANCED PRACTICE REGISTERED NURSE NOT GIVING TREATMENT OR STOPPING TREATMENT WHICH WOULD KEEP YOU ALIVE.

4. UNLESS YOU SPECIFY A SHORTER PERIOD IN THIS DOCUMENT, THIS POWER WILL EXIST INDEFINITELY FROM THE DATE YOU EXECUTE THIS DOCUMENT AND, IF YOU ARE UNABLE TO MAKE HEALTH CARE DECISIONS FOR YOURSELF, THIS POWER WILL CONTINUE TO EXIST UNTIL THE TIME WHEN YOU BECOME ABLE TO MAKE HEALTH CARE DECISIONS FOR YOURSELF.

5. NOTWITHSTANDING THIS DOCUMENT, YOU HAVE THE RIGHT TO MAKE MEDICAL AND OTHER HEALTH CARE DECISIONS FOR YOURSELF SO LONG AS YOU CAN GIVE INFORMED CONSENT WITH RESPECT TO THE PARTICULAR DECISION. IN ADDITION, NO TREATMENT MAY BE GIVEN TO YOU OVER YOUR OBJECTION, AND HEALTH CARE NECESSARY TO KEEP YOU ALIVE MAY NOT BE STOPPED IF YOU OBJECT.

6. YOU HAVE THE RIGHT TO DECIDE WHERE YOU LIVE, EVEN AS YOU AGE. DECISIONS ABOUT WHERE YOU LIVE ARE PERSONAL. SOME PEOPLE LIVE AT HOME WITH SUPPORT, WHILE OTHERS MOVE TO ASSISTED LIVING FACILITIES OR FACILITIES FOR SKILLED NURSING. IN SOME CASES, PEOPLE ARE MOVED TO FACILITIES WITH LOCKED DOORS TO PREVENT PEOPLE WITH COGNITIVE DISORDERS FROM LEAVING OR GETTING LOST OR TO PROVIDE ASSISTANCE TO PEOPLE WHO REQUIRE A HIGHER LEVEL OF CARE. YOU SHOULD DISCUSS WITH THE PERSON DESIGNATED IN THIS DOCUMENT YOUR DESIRES ABOUT WHERE YOU LIVE AS YOU AGE OR IF YOUR HEALTH DECLINES. YOU HAVE THE RIGHT TO DETERMINE WHETHER TO AUTHORIZE THE PERSON DESIGNATED IN THIS DOCUMENT TO MAKE DECISIONS FOR YOU ABOUT WHERE YOU LIVE WHEN YOU ARE NO LONGER CAPABLE OF MAKING THAT DECISION. IF YOU DO NOT PROVIDE SUCH AUTHORIZATION TO THE PERSON DESIGNATED IN THIS DOCUMENT, THAT PERSON MAY NOT BE ABLE TO ASSIST YOU TO MOVE TO A MORE SUPPORTIVE LIVING ARRANGEMENT WITHOUT OBTAINING APPROVAL THROUGH A JUDICIAL PROCESS.

7. YOU HAVE THE RIGHT TO REVOKE THE APPOINTMENT OF THE PERSON DESIGNATED IN THIS DOCUMENT TO MAKE HEALTH CARE DECISIONS FOR YOU BY NOTIFYING THAT PERSON OF THE REVOCATION ORALLY OR IN WRITING.

8. YOU HAVE THE RIGHT TO REVOKE THE AUTHORITY GRANTED TO THE PERSON DESIGNATED IN THIS DOCUMENT TO MAKE HEALTH CARE DECISIONS FOR YOU BY NOTIFYING THE TREATING PHYSICIAN, ADVANCED PRACTICE REGISTERED NURSE, HOSPITAL OR OTHER PROVIDER OF HEALTH CARE ORALLY OR IN WRITING.

9. THE PERSON DESIGNATED IN THIS DOCUMENT TO MAKE HEALTH CARE DECISIONS FOR YOU HAS THE RIGHT TO EXAMINE YOUR MEDICAL RECORDS AND TO CONSENT TO THEIR DISCLOSURE UNLESS YOU LIMIT THIS RIGHT IN THIS DOCUMENT.

10. THIS DOCUMENT REVOKES ANY PRIOR DURABLE POWER OF ATTORNEY FOR HEALTH CARE.

11. IF THERE IS ANYTHING IN THIS DOCUMENT THAT YOU DO NOT UNDERSTAND, YOU SHOULD ASK A LAWYER TO EXPLAIN IT TO YOU.

12. YOU MAY REQUEST THAT THE NEVADA SECRETARY OF STATE ELECTRONICALLY STORE WITH THE NEVADA LOCKBOX A COPY OF THIS DOCUMENT TO ALLOW ACCESS BY AN AUTHORIZED PROVIDER OF HEALTH CARE AS DEFINED IN NRS 629.031.

1. DESIGNATION OF HEALTH CARE AGENT.

I, _____
                    (insert your name) do hereby designate and appoint:

Name: _____

Address: _____

Telephone Number: _____

as my agent to make health care decisions for me as authorized in this document.

(Insert the name and address of the person you wish to designate as your agent to make health care decisions for you. Unless the person is also your spouse, legal guardian or the person most closely related to you by blood, none of the following may be designated as your agent: (1) your treating provider of health care; (2) an employee of your treating provider of health care; (3) an operator of a health care facility; or (4) an employee of an operator of a health care facility.)

2. CREATION OF DURABLE POWER OF ATTORNEY FOR HEALTH CARE.

By this document I intend to create a durable power of attorney by appointing the person designated above to make health care decisions for me. This power of attorney shall not be affected by my subsequent incapacity.

3. GENERAL STATEMENT OF AUTHORITY GRANTED.

In the event that I am incapable of giving informed consent with respect to health care decisions, I hereby grant to the agent named above full power and authority: to make health care decisions for me before or after my death, including consent, refusal of consent or withdrawal of consent to any care, treatment, service or procedure to maintain, diagnose or treat a physical or mental condition; to request, review and receive any information, verbal or written, regarding my physical or mental health, including, without limitation, medical and hospital records; to execute on my behalf any releases or other documents that may be required to obtain medical care and/or medical and hospital records, EXCEPT any power to enter into any arbitration agreements or execute any arbitration clauses in connection with admission to any health care facility including any skilled nursing facility; and subject only to the limitations and special provisions, if any, set forth in paragraph 4 or 6.

4. SPECIAL PROVISIONS AND LIMITATIONS.

(Your agent is not permitted to consent to any of the following: commitment to or placement in a mental health treatment facility, convulsive treatment, psychosurgery, sterilization or abortion. If there are any other types of treatment or placement that you do not want your agent's authority to give consent for or other restrictions you wish to place on his or her agent's authority, you should list them in the space below. If you do not write any limitations, your agent will have the broad powers to make health care decisions on your behalf which are set forth in paragraph 3, except to the extent that there are limits provided by law.)

In exercising the authority under this durable power of attorney for health care, the authority of my agent is subject to the following special provisions and limitations:

_____

_____

5. DURATION.

I understand that this power of attorney will exist indefinitely from the date I execute this document unless I establish a shorter time. If I am unable to make health care decisions for myself when this power of attorney expires, the authority I have granted my agent will continue to exist until the time when I become able to make health care decisions for myself.

(IF APPLICABLE)

I wish to have this power of attorney end on the following date: _____, 20___

6. STATEMENT OF DESIRES CONCERNING TREATMENT.

(With respect to decisions to withhold or withdraw life-sustaining treatment, your agent must make health care decisions that are consistent with your known desires. You can, but are not required to, indicate your desires below. If your desires are unknown, your agent has the duty to act in your best interests; and, under some circumstances, a judicial proceeding may be necessary so that a court can determine the health care decision that is in your best interests. If you wish to indicate your desires, you may INITIAL the statement or statements that reflect your desires and/or write your own statements in the space below.)

(If the statement reflects your desires, initial the box next to the statement.)

A. I desire that my life be prolonged to the greatest extent possible, without regard to my condition, the chances I have for recovery or long-term survival, or the cost of the procedures. [   ]

B. If I am in a coma which my doctors or advanced practice registered nurses have reasonably concluded is irreversible, I desire that life-sustaining or prolonging treatments not be used. [   ]

C. If I have an incurable or terminal condition or illness and no reasonable hope of long-term recovery or survival, I desire that life-sustaining or prolonging treatments not be used. [   ]

D. Withholding or withdrawal of artificial nutrition and hydration may result in death by starvation or dehydration. I want to receive or continue receiving artificial nutrition and hydration by way of the gastrointestinal tract after all other treatment is withheld. [   ]

E. I do not desire treatment to be provided and/or continued if the burdens of the treatment outweigh the expected benefits. My agent is to consider the relief of suffering, the preservation or restoration of functioning, and the quality as well as the extent of the possible extension of my life. [   ]

F. If I have an incurable or terminal condition, including late stage dementia, or illness and no reasonable hope of long-term recovery or survival, I desire my attending physician to administer any medication to alleviate suffering without regard that the medication is likely to cause addiction or reduce the extension of my life. [   ]

(If you wish to change your answer, you may do so by drawing an "X" through the answer you do not want, and circling the answer you prefer.)

Other or Additional Statements of Desires: _____

_____

_____

7. STATEMENT OF DESIRES CONCERNING LIVING ARRANGEMENTS

A. I desire to live in my home as long as it is safe and my medical needs can be met. My agent may arrange for a natural person, employee of an agency or provider of community-based services to come into my home to provide care for me. When it is no longer safe for me to live in my home, I authorize my agent to place me in a facility or home that can provide any medical assistance and support in my activities of daily living that I require. Before being placed in such a facility or home, I wish for my agent to discuss and share information concerning the placement with me. [   ]

B. I desire to live in my home for as long as possible without regard for my medical needs, personal safety or ability to engage in activities of daily living. My agent may arrange for a natural person, an employee of an agency or a provider of community-based services to come into my home and provide care for me. I understand that, before I may be placed in a facility or home other than the home in which I currently reside, a guardian must be appointed for me. [   ]

(If you wish to change your answer, you may do so by drawing an "X" through the answer you do not want, and circling the answer you prefer.)

Other or Additional Statements of Desires: _____

_____

8. DESIGNATION OF ALTERNATE AGENT.

(You are not required to designate any alternative agent but you may do so. Any alternative agent you designate will be able to make the same health care decisions as the agent designated in paragraph 1, page 2, in the event that he or she is unable or unwilling to act as your agent. Also, if the agent designated in paragraph 1 is your spouse, his or her designation as your agent is automatically revoked by law if your marriage is dissolved.)

If the person designated in paragraph 1 as my agent is unable to make health care decisions for me, then I designate the following persons to serve as my agent to make health care decisions for me as authorized in this document, such persons to serve in the order listed below:

A. First Alternative Agent
Name: _____
Address: _____
Telephone Number: _____

B. Second Alternative Agent
Name: _____
Address: _____
Telephone Number: _____

9. PRIOR DESIGNATIONS REVOKED.
I revoke any prior durable power of attorney for health care.

10. WAIVER OF CONFLICT OF INTEREST.

If my designated agent is my spouse or is one of my children, then I waive any conflict of interest in carrying out the provisions of this Durable Power of Attorney for Health Care that said spouse or child may have by reason of the fact that he or she may be a beneficiary of my estate.

11. CHALLENGES.

If the legality of any provision of this Durable Power of Attorney for Health Care is questioned by my physician, my advanced practice registered nurse, my agent or a third party, then my agent is authorized to commence an action for declaratory judgment as to the legality of the provision in question. The cost of any such action is to be paid from my estate. This Durable Power of Attorney for Health Care must be construed and interpreted in accordance with the laws of the State of Nevada.

12. NOMINATION OF GUARDIAN.

If, after execution of this Durable Power of Attorney for Health Care, proceedings seeking an adjudication of incapacity are initiated either for my estate or my person, I hereby nominate as my guardian or conservator for consideration by the court my agent herein named, in the order named.

13. RELEASE OF INFORMATION.

I agree to, authorize and allow full release of information by any government agency, medical provider, business, creditor or third party who may have information pertaining to my health care, to my agent named herein, pursuant to the Health Insurance Portability and Accountability Act of 1996, Public Law 104-191, as amended, and applicable regulations.

(YOU MUST DATE AND SIGN THIS POWER OF ATTORNEY)

I sign my name to this Durable Power of Attorney for Health Care on _____, 20___ (date) at _____(city), Nevada.

_____
(Signature)

(THIS POWER OF ATTORNEY WILL NOT BE VALID FOR MAKING HEALTH CARE DECISIONS UNLESS IT IS EITHER (1) SIGNED BY AT LEAST TWO QUALIFIED WITNESSES WHO ARE PERSONALLY KNOWN TO YOU AND WHO ARE PRESENT WHEN YOU SIGN OR ACKNOWLEDGE YOUR SIGNATURE OR (2) ACKNOWLEDGED BEFORE A NOTARY PUBLIC.)

CERTIFICATE OF ACKNOWLEDGMENT
OF NOTARY PUBLIC

(You may use acknowledgment before a notary public instead of the statement of witnesses.)

State of Nevada   }
County of _____ }ss.

On this ___ day of _____, in the year ____, before me,_____ (here insert name of notary public) personally appeared _____ (here insert name of principal) personally known to me (or proved to me on the basis of satisfactory evidence) to be the person whose name is subscribed to this instrument, and acknowledged that he or she executed it.

NOTARY SEAL

_____
(Signature of Notary Public)

STATEMENT OF WITNESSES
(You may use a statement of witnesses instead of an acknowledgment before a notary public).

(You should carefully read and follow this witnessing procedure. This document will not be valid unless you comply with the witnessing procedure. If you elect to use witnesses instead of having this document notarized, you must use two qualified adult witnesses. None of the following may be used as a witness: (1) a person you designate as the agent; (2) a provider of health care; (3) an employee of a provider of health care; (4) the operator of a health care facility; or (5) an employee of an operator of a health care facility. At least one of the witnesses must make the additional declaration set out following the place where the witnesses sign.)

I declare under penalty of perjury that the principal is personally known to me, that the principal signed or acknowledged this durable power of attorney in my presence, that the principal appears to be of sound mind and under no duress, fraud or undue influence, that I am not the person appointed as agent by this document and that I am not a provider of health care, an employee of a provider of health care, the operator of a health care facility or an employee of an operator of a health care facility.

Signature: _____   Residence Address: _____

Print Name: _____   _____

Date: _____   _____

Signature: _____   Residence Address: _____

Print Name: _____   _____

Date: _____   _____

(AT LEAST ONE OF THE ABOVE WITNESSES MUST ALSO SIGN THE FOLLOWING DECLARATION.)

I declare under penalty of perjury that I am not related to the principal by blood, marriage or adoption and that to the best of my knowledge, I am not entitled to any part of the estate of the principal upon the death of the principal under a will now existing or by operation of law.

Signature: _____

Signature: _____

Names: _____   Address: _____

Print Name: _____   _____

Date: _____   _____

COPIES: You should retain an executed copy of this document and give one to your agent. The power of attorney should be available so a copy may be given to your providers of health care. This includes requesting the Nevada Secretary of State to electronically store this document with the Nevada Lockbox to allow access by authorized providers of healthcare.

- - OPTIONAL HANDMADE WALLET CARD - -
(cut out and fill out and then keep in handy place to show any health care provider)

ATTN: NEVADA HEALTH CARE PROVIDERS
Name:_____

I have the following Advanced Directives:

_____ **Durable Power of Attorney For Health Care Decisions**

_____ **Living Will Declaration**

_____ **Do Not Resuscitate**

For information contact this person:

_____
(Name and Phone Number)

ATTN: NEVADA HEALTH CARE PROVIDERS
Name:_____

I have the following Advanced Directives:

_____ **Durable Power of Attorney For Health Care Decisions**

_____ **Living Will Declaration**

_____ **Do Not Resuscitate**

For information contact this person:

_____
(Name and Phone Number)

ATTN: NEVADA HEALTH CARE PROVIDERS
Name:_____

I have the following Advanced Directives:

_____ **Durable Power of Attorney For Health Care Decisions**

_____ **Living Will Declaration**

_____ **Do Not Resuscitate**

For information contact this person:

_____
(Name and Phone Number)

ATTN: NEVADA HEALTH CARE PROVIDERS
Name:_____

I have the following Advanced Directives:

_____ **Durable Power of Attorney For Health Care Decisions**

_____ **Living Will Declaration**

_____ **Do Not Resuscitate**

For information contact this person:

_____
(Name and Phone Number)

CHAPTER 13
FORM 7: LIVING WILL DECLARATION

IN FORM CAN SAY TO STOP HEALTH CARE IF LATER HEALTH GETS BAD

This form lets a person do serious act of saying stop health care if <u>later</u> doctors think it likely won't help. The form is long and is mostly used <u>in</u> hospitals or similar places. This is a statutory form found in state law.

CAN STAY STOP MOST CARE IF LATER DOCTORS SAY IT LIKELY WON'T HELP

Care that is needed to keep people living is called "life-sustaining" care. This Chapter's form can do the serious act of saying stop this care <u>if later doctors think an incapacitated person has bad health and further health</u> artificial feeding and water to be withheld. <u>In Nevada this Living Will form is rarely done</u>, since rarely do these issues matter, this form can cause legal issues, and most people trust family or Health Care Agent to consider many factors and make wise decisions. Also, as the previous Chapter said many people choose to handle life-sustaining care issues in the Durable Power Of Attorney For Health Care Decisions form by initialing a few options and then handwriting in a paragraph about stopping care.

SIGN FORM WITH 2 WITNESSES AND CAN FILE IN NEVADA LOCKBOX

The form must be signed in front of 2 persons acting as witnesses who then sign too. In the form everyone should also write their addresses. A person to be a witness must be at least age 18, not involved in any way with a place giving health care to the person doing the form, not named in any form as Health Care Agent, and not someone entitled like by Will to any part of the estate, money, or property of person doing the form (so usually no close family). Once it is done the form usually is shown to all places that may give care to put in the person's medical file to follow. To cancel the form a person usually should clearly tell all places shown the form that it is now canceled.

CAN FILE FORM IN "NEVADA LOCKBOX" AT SECRETARY OF STATE'S OFFICE

As the last Chapter said a form like this can be filed in the "Nevada Lockbox" system run by the Nevada Secretary of State. See **www.nvsos.gov**. This lets people file health care forms so hospitals and other places can look up if a person has done forms. After filing people will be mailed a "Lockbox wallet card". But most people skip this and just make sure hospitals and other places are directly shown any forms.

LIVING WILL
DECLARATION

(Nevada Revised Statutes 449A.436)

If I should have an incurable and irreversible condition that, without the administration of
life-sustaining treatment, will, in the opinion of my attending physician or attending
advanced practice registered nurse, cause my death within a relatively short time, and I am
no longer able to make decisions regarding my medical treatment, I direct my attending
physician or attending advanced practice registered nurse, pursuant to NRS 449A.400 to
449A.481, inclusive, **to withhold or withdraw treatment that only prolongs the
process of dying and is not necessary for my comfort or to alleviate pain**.

If you wish to include this statement (below) in this declaration, you must INITIAL the
statement in the box provided:

Withholding or withdrawal of artificial nutrition and hydration may result in
death by starvation or dehydration. Initial this box if you want to receive or
continue receiving artificial nutrition and hydration by way of the gastrointestinal tract after all other treatment is withheld pursuant to this declaration.

Signed this ____ day of _____, 20___ .

Signature _____

Address _____

The declarant voluntarily signed this writing in my presence.

Witness _____

Address _____

Witness _____

Address _____

CHAPTER 14
FORM 8: DO-NOT-RESUSCITATE

FORM LETS PERSON IMMEDIATELY SAY TO NOT TRY RESUSCITATION

The Do-Not-Resuscitate form, often called the "DNR" form, does serious act of saying <u>immediately from now on</u> do not try to resuscitate a person. The form is short so can be read fast like by paramedics and be used outside hospitals or similar place, but it can be used in these places too.

FORM SAYS TO IMMEDIATELY NO LONGER TRY RESUSCITATION LIKE C.P.R.

In the form a person can say <u>starting immediately from now on</u> no longer try to <u>resuscitate</u> by trying to help the heart or breathing, and mostly this means cardio-pulmonary resuscitation (C.P.R.) won't be tried. This also means some machines to help with the heart and breathing won't be used. A person with capacity still thinking fine can override this form like by saying this to doctors or not showing the form to paramedics. <u>But this form is rarely done, usually only by people with a terminal condition or similar serious situation</u>. A person's doctor or similar professional must sign the form and they can help explain all about this form. Note, instead of this Do-Not-Resuscitate form a similar "Provider Order for Life-Sustaining Treatment" form is often used inside Nevada hospitals or similar places and can be used outside these places too. The P.O.L.S.T. form covers far more treatments than just resuscitation and usually is on pink paper.

DOCTOR AND PERSON SIGN THE FORM AND CAN FILE IN LOCKBOX

The Do-Not-Resuscitate form must be signed by a doctor or similar health professional, and by person doing the form or someone with authority for them, and then mailed in. As doctors know and can help with there is a different "Out Of Hospital" DNR form to do if a person is not yet in a hospital or similar place. After this form is filed people will get by mail a "DNR" wallet card that all health care providers including paramedics will follow if they see it. People often also quickly show the form or wallet card to places that may give care to make it part of a person's medical file. Some people keeps copies handy to show paramedics or other people who may want to give health care, like on a bedside table, on a refrigerator, in a wallet placed to be visible, on a lanyard, or some people get from doctors a "Nevada DNR" bracelet. To cancel things a person usually tells all places shown the form it is canceled and shouldn't be followed.

CAN FILE FORM IN "NEVADA LOCKBOX" AT SECRETARY OF STATE'S OFFICE

As previous Chapters said a form like this can be filed in the "Nevada Lockbox" system run by the Nevada Secretary of State. See **www.nvsos.gov**. This lets people file health care forms so hospitals and other places can look up if a person has done forms. But most people skip this and just make sure hospitals and other places are directly shown any forms.

State of Nevada
Do-Not-Resuscitate Identification
Application – Adult

Patient Information (Please Print or Type)

Name:_____

Last   First   Middle

Address:_____ Phone #:_____

Street   City   State   Zip

Birthdate:_____ Gender: ☐ Male   ☐ Female

A. Patient's Statement

I, the above named patient, am capable of making an informed decision and **do not wish to receive life-resuscitating treatment in the event of a cardiac or respiratory arrest.** Therefore, I **direct Emergency Medical Services personnel to withhold life-resuscitating treatment.** I verify that I have informed each member of my immediate family whose whereabouts are known to me, and/or my legal guardian or caretaker of my decision to apply for a Do-Not-Resuscitate Identification.

Patient's Signature:_____ Date:_____

B. Agent's Statement

I am the above named patient's agent (with durable power of attorney for healthcare decisions pursuant to NRS 449.786 to 449.900, inclusive). The patient does not wish to receive life-resuscitating treatment in the event of a cardiac or respiratory arrest. **I direct Emergency Medical Services personnel to withhold life-resuscitating treatment in the event of a cardiac or respiratory arrest.**

Agent's Name (Print):_____

Last   First   Middle

Agent's Address:_____ Phone #:_____

Street   City   State   Zip

Agent's Signature:_____ Date:_____

Attending Physician's Statement

As required by Nevada Revised Statutes (NRS) 450B.520(2), I certify that I am the above patient's attending physician/physician who has primary responsibility for the treatment and care of the patient and that the patient suffers from a terminal condition. The patient is capable of making an informed decision or, when he/she was capable of making an informed decision, he/she executed a written directive that life-resuscitating treatment be withheld under certain circumstances, or a durable power of attorney for health care decisions pursuant to NRS 449.786 to 449.900, inclusive, or he/she was issued a Do-Not-Resuscitate order pursuant to NRS 450B.510.

Attending Physician's Name (Print):_____ Phone #:_____

Last   First

Agent's Physician's Signature:_____ NV License #:_____

Office use only:

Received:_____ Issued:_____ By:_____ DNR ID #_____

State of Nevada

Do-Not-Resuscitate

Identification

Application

Adult
(18+ years of age)

Division of Public and Behavioral Health
Emergency Medical Systems

4150 Technology Way, Suite 101
Carson City, NV 89706
775-687-7590

The 1997 Legislature enacted Assembly Bill (AB) 29, allowing "qualified patients" to apply for a DNR Identification. AB 29 subsequently was codified as Nevada Revised Statute NRS 450B.400 to 450B.590, inclusive. DNR Identification instructs pre-hospital emergency medical services personnel to withhold life-resuscitating treatment in the event of cardiac or respiratory arrest. EMS personnel will provide appropriate emergency medical and supportive care to patients with DNR Identification if the patient is not experiencing cardiac or respiratory arrest.

A "qualified patient" is a patient who has executed a declaration, in accordance with NRS 450B.470, governing the withholding or withdrawal of life-sustaining treatment and who has been determined by his attending physician to be a terminal condition.

DNR Identification will be a card and document issued by the Division of Public and Behavioral Health signifying the person is a qualified patient who wishes not to be resuscitated in the event of cardiac or respiratory arrest. NRS 450B.410.

Life-resuscitating treatment means cardiopulmonary resuscitation (CPR) or any of it components including chest compressions, defibrillation, cardioversion, assisted ventilation, airway intubation and administration of cardiotonic medications.

Patients applying for DNR Identification should fully discuss their decision with their family members or caretakers. Family members or caretakers are generally the ones who call EMS when the patient needs medical assistance. Being aware and supportive of the patient's wishes in this area allows them to appropriately advise EMS personnel responding to care for the patient.

Applicant Instructions

1. Provide the information required in the 'Patient Information' section of the application.

2. Sign and date the 'Patient's Statement' or Agent's Statement' section of the application.

3. Have your attending physician complete and sign the 'Attending Physician's Statement' section of the application.

4. Include a check or money order in the amount of $5, payable to the Division of Public and Behavioral Health, with the completed application

5. Mail the completed application to:

   Emergency Medical Systems
   4150 Technology Way, Suite 101
   Carson City, NV 89706

Attending Physician's Instructions

1. Provide your name, phone number and NV license number; and

2. Sign the 'Attending Physician's Statement' where indicated.

For additional information please call:
Division of Public and Behavioral Health
Emergency Medical Systems
775-687-7590

CHAPTER 15
FORM 9: STATUTORY FORM POWER OF ATTORNEY

FORM LETS POWER BE GIVEN OVER PROPERTY, MONEY, AND MORE

This form lets person during life give power to someone trusted over property, money, and other things. This Chapter's form is a statutory form found in state law for people to find and use if they want.

FORM GIVES POWER TO LET SOMEONE CONTROL PROPERTY AND MONEY

The form lets a person give power to someone trusted over money, property, records, and other things. The person giving power is often called the "Principal" and person getting power called "Agent" (or "Attorney-in-Fact") who is often a spouse, relative, or friend. An "Alternate Agent" can be named just in case needed. This form can let someone help if a person is sick, busy, or away. Using this form may avoid more serious legal actions like Guardianship or other court action. The Agent might do helpful things for a person like use funds in their accounts, pay bills, buy/sell items, sign contracts, hire workers, borrow, get records, take legal actions, file taxes, and handle insurance. A person who isn't incapacitated can overrule or fire their Agent. The form is "durable" so it isn't affected by later disability or incapacity of Principal till they die. Agent when signing should be like, for example: "Luke Ian Smith by Ann Sue Hart as Agent using a Power of Attorney". Note, under Nevada law banks and similar parties sometimes can refuse or delay in following a Power of Attorney form, so often people communicate in advance to see what kind of form is wanted.

IN THE FORM CAN PICK POWERS TO GIVE AND WRITE INSTRUCTIONS

In the form a person can initial lines to show which powers they want to give by initial certain form lines. But often people give most or all powers since a bank or other place may refuse to follow Agent's instructions if their power is not clear. In the form instructions for the Agent can be added but this is often skipped to avoid the risk of making Agent's powers not clear.

DUE TO RISKS INCLUDING FRAUD MANY SKIP FORM OR CONSULT A LAWYER

Many people skip the form or first see a lawyer. Using this form s risky and can lead to harm since the Agent can buy unneeded or costly items, commit fraud or similar, or by carelessness allow other harms. Agents have a duty to act reasonably for Principal but may be out of money later so can't pay for any losses. Usually banks or others can't be blamed for obeying an Agent. The law is complex and basic acts may be fine like paying bills, getting records, or moving funds around, but some acts may be improper like making gifts, risky investments, or do unusual things. It is best if a person not their Agent does anything unusual.

PERSON SIGNS FORM IN FRONT OF A NOTARY

The form must be signed by the person doing the form in front of a notary who then notarizes the form. Once done some cautious people quickly show it to banks and other places to clearly say to follow it later. Usually the form is given to the person named as Agent to hold and use if needed. To cancel the form a person usually takes back copies from the Agent and maybe tells places that saw the form it's canceled. Note, in rare cases to use this form if a person is very sick and resides in a hospital, residential facility for groups, facility for skilled nursing, or home for individual residential care then a doctor may need to do a "Certificate Of Competency To Executor Power Of Attorney".

STATUTORY FORM POWER OF ATTORNEY
(Nevada Revised Statutes 162A.620)

THIS IS AN IMPORTANT LEGAL DOCUMENT. IT CREATES A DURABLE POWER OF ATTORNEY FOR FINANCIAL MATTERS. BEFORE EXECUTING THIS DOCUMENT, YOU SHOULD KNOW THESE IMPORTANT FACTS:

1.   THIS DOCUMENT GIVES THE PERSON YOU DESIGNATE AS YOUR AGENT THE POWER TO MAKE DECISIONS CONCERNING YOUR PROPERTY FOR YOU. YOUR AGENT WILL BE ABLE TO MAKE DECISIONS AND ACT WITH RESPECT TO YOUR PROPERTY (INCLUDING YOUR MONEY) WHETHER OR NOT YOU ARE ABLE TO ACT FOR YOURSELF.

2.   THIS POWER OF ATTORNEY BECOMES EFFECTIVE IMMEDIATELY UNLESS YOU STATE OTHERWISE IN THE SPECIAL INSTRUCTIONS.

3.   THIS POWER OF ATTORNEY DOES NOT AUTHORIZE THE AGENT TO MAKE HEALTH CARE DECISIONS FOR YOU.

4.   THE PERSON YOU DESIGNATE IN THIS DOCUMENT HAS A DUTY TO ACT CONSISTENT WITH YOUR DESIRES AS STATED IN THIS DOCUMENT OR OTHERWISE MADE KNOWN OR, IF YOUR DESIRES ARE UNKNOWN, TO ACT IN YOUR BEST INTERESTS.

5.   YOU SHOULD SELECT SOMEONE YOU TRUST TO SERVE AS YOUR AGENT. UNLESS YOU SPECIFY OTHERWISE, GENERALLY THE AGENT'S AUTHORITY WILL CONTINUE UNTIL YOU DIE OR REVOKE THE POWER OF ATTORNEY OR THE AGENT RESIGNS OR IS UNABLE TO ACT FOR YOU.

6.   YOUR AGENT IS ENTITLED TO REASONABLE COMPENSATION UNLESS YOU STATE OTHERWISE IN THE SPECIAL INSTRUCTIONS.

7.   THIS FORM PROVIDES FOR DESIGNATION OF ONE AGENT. IF YOU WISH TO NAME MORE THAN ONE AGENT YOU MAY NAME A CO-AGENT IN THE SPECIAL INSTRUCTIONS. CO-AGENTS ARE NOT REQUIRED TO ACT TOGETHER UNLESS YOU INCLUDE THAT REQUIREMENT IN THE SPECIAL INSTRUCTIONS.

8.   IF YOUR AGENT IS UNABLE OR UNWILLING TO ACT FOR YOU, YOUR POWER OF ATTORNEY WILL END UNLESS YOU HAVE NAMED A SUCCESSOR AGENT. YOU MAY ALSO NAME A SECOND SUCCESSOR AGENT.

9.   YOU HAVE THE RIGHT TO REVOKE THE AUTHORITY GRANTED TO THE PERSON DESIGNATED IN THIS DOCUMENT.

10.   THIS DOCUMENT REVOKES ANY PRIOR DURABLE POWER OF ATTORNEY.

11.   IF THERE IS ANYTHING IN THIS DOCUMENT THAT YOU DO NOT UNDERSTAND, YOU SHOULD ASK A LAWYER TO EXPLAIN IT TO YOU.

1.   DESIGNATION OF AGENT.

I, _____

(insert your name) do hereby designate and appoint:

Name: _____

Address: _____

Telephone Number: _____

as my agent to make decisions for me and in my name, place and stead and for my use and benefit and to exercise the powers as authorized in this document.

2. DESIGNATION OF ALTERNATE AGENT.

(You are not required to designate any alternative agent but you may do so. Any alternative agent you designate will be able to make the same decisions as the agent designated above in the event that he or she is unable or unwilling to act as your agent. Also, if the agent designated in paragraph 1 is your spouse, his or her designation as your agent is automatically revoked by law if your marriage is dissolved.)

If my agent is unable or unwilling to act for me, then I designate the following person(s) to serve as my agent as authorized in this document, such person(s) to serve in the order listed below:

A. First Alternative Agent

Name: _____

Address: _____

Telephone Number: _____

B. Second Alternative Agent

Name: _____

Address: _____

Telephone Number: _____

3. OTHER POWERS OF ATTORNEY.

This Power of Attorney is intended to, and does, revoke any prior Power of Attorney for financial matters I have previously executed.

4. NOMINATION OF GUARDIAN.

If, after execution of this Power of Attorney, proceedings seeking an adjudication of incapacity are initiated either for my estate or my person, I hereby nominate as my guardian or conservator for consideration by the court my agent herein named, in the order named.

5. GRANT OF GENERAL AUTHORITY.

I grant my agent and any successor agent(s) general authority to act for me with respect to the following subjects:

(INITIAL each subject you want to include in the agent's general authority. If you wish to grant general authority over all of the subjects you may initial "All Preceding Subjects" instead of initialing each subject.)

|_____| Real Property

|_____| Tangible Personal Property

|_____| Stocks and Bonds

|_____| Commodities and Options

|_____| Banks and Other Financial Institutions

|_____| Safe Deposit Boxes

|_____| Operation of Entity or Business

|_____| Insurance and Annuities

|_____| Estates, Trusts and Other Beneficial Interests

|_____| Legal Affairs, Claims and Litigation

|_____| Personal Maintenance

|_____| Benefits from Governmental Programs or Civil or Military Service

|_____| Retirement Plans

|_____| Taxes

|_____| All Preceding Subjects

6. GRANT OF SPECIFIC AUTHORITY.

My agent MAY NOT do any of the following specific acts for me UNLESS I have INITIALED the specific authority listed below:

(CAUTION: Granting any of the following will give your agent the authority to take actions that could significantly reduce your property or change how your property is distributed at your death. INITIAL ONLY the specific authority you WANT to give your agent.)

|_____| Create, amend, revoke or terminate an inter vivos, family, living, irrevocable or revocable trust
|_____| Make a gift, subject to the limitations of NRS and any special instructions in this Power of Attorney
|_____| Create or change rights of survivorship
|_____| Create or change a beneficiary designation
|_____| Waive the principal's right to be a beneficiary of a joint and survivor annuity, including a survivor benefit under a retirement plan
|_____| Exercise fiduciary powers that the principal has authority to delegate
|_____| Disclaim or refuse an interest in property, including a power of appointment

7. EXPRESSION OF INTENT CONCERNING LIVING ARRANGEMENTS.

|_____| It is my intention to live in my home as long as it is safe and my medical needs can be met. My agent may arrange for a natural person, employee of an agency or provider of community-based services to come into my home to provide care for me. When it is no longer safe for me to live in my home, I authorize my agent to place me in a facility or home that can provide any medical assistance and support in my activities of daily living that I require. Before being placed in such a facility or home, I wish for my agent to discuss and share information concerning the placement with me.

|_____| It is my intention to live in my home for as long as possible without regard for my medical needs, personal safety or ability to engage in activities of daily living. My agent may arrange for a natural person, an employee of an agency or a provider of community-based services to come into my home and provide care for me. I understand that, before I may be placed in a facility or home other than the home in which I currently reside, a guardian must be appointed for me.

|_____| I desire for my agent to take the following actions relating to my care:

_____
_____
_____

8. LIMITATION ON AGENT'S AUTHORITY.

An agent that is not my spouse MAY NOT use my property to benefit the agent or a person to whom the agent owes an obligation of support unless I have included that authority in the Special Instructions.

9. SPECIAL INSTRUCTIONS OR OTHER OR ADDITIONAL AUTHORITY GRANTED TO AGENT: _____

_____

10. AUTHORITY OF PRINCIPAL.

Except as otherwise expressly provided in this Power of Attorney, the authority of a principal to act on his or her own behalf continues after executing this Power of Attorney and any decision or instruction communicated by the principal supersedes any inconsistent decision or instruction communicated by an agent appointed pursuant to this Power of Attorney.

11. DURABILITY AND EFFECTIVE DATE. (INITIAL the clause(s) that applies.)

|_____| DURABLE. This Power of Attorney shall not be affected by my subsequent disability or incapacity.

|_____| SPRINGING POWER. It is my intention and direction that my designated agent, and any person or entity that my designated agent may transact business with on my behalf, may rely on a written medical opinion issued by a licensed medical doctor stating that I am disabled or incapacitated, and incapable of managing my affairs, and that said medical opinion shall establish whether or not I am under a disability for the purpose of establishing the authority of my designated agent to act in accordance with this Power of Attorney.

|_____| I wish to have this Power of Attorney become effective on the following date:_____

|_____| I wish to have this Power of Attorney end on the following date: _____

12. THIRD PARTY PROTECTION.

Third parties may rely upon the validity of this Power of Attorney or a copy and the representations of my agent as to all matters relating to any power granted to my agent, and no person or agency who relies upon the representation of my agent, or the authority granted by my agent, shall incur any liability to me or my estate as a result of permitting my agent to exercise any power unless a third party knows or has reason to know this Power of Attorney has terminated or is invalid.

13. RELEASE OF INFORMATION.

I agree to, authorize and allow full release of information, by any government agency, business, creditor or third party who may have information pertaining to my assets or income, to my agent named herein.

14. SIGNATURE AND ACKNOWLEDGMENT. YOU MUST DATE AND SIGN THIS POWER OF ATTORNEY. THIS POWER OF ATTORNEY WILL NOT BE VALID UNLESS IT IS ACKNOWLEDGED BEFORE A NOTARY PUBLIC.

I sign my name to this Power of Attorney on _____(date) at _____(city), Nevada.

_____
(Signature)

CERTIFICATE OF ACKNOWLEDGMENT OF NOTARY PUBLIC

(You may use acknowledgment before a notary public instead of the statement of witnesses.)

State of Nevada   }
                          } ss.
County of _____ }

On this __ day of _____, in the year 20__, before me, _____ (here insert name of notary public) personally appeared _____ (here insert name of principal) personally known to me (or proved to me on the basis of satisfactory evidence) to be the person whose name is subscribed to this instrument, and acknowledged that he or she executed it.

NOTARY SEAL

_____
(Signature of Notary Public)

IMPORTANT INFORMATION FOR AGENT

1. Agent's Duties. When you accept the authority granted under this Power of Attorney, a special legal relationship is created between you and the principal. This relationship imposes upon you legal duties that continue until you resign or the Power of Attorney is terminated or revoked. You must:

(a) Do what you know the principal reasonably expects you to do with the principal's property or, if you do not know the principal's expectations, act in the principal's best interest;

(b) Act in good faith;

(c) Do nothing beyond the authority granted in this Power of Attorney; and

(d) Disclose your identity as an agent whenever you act for the principal by writing or printing the name of the principal and signing your own name as "agent" in the following manner:

(Principal's Name) by (Your Signature) as Agent

2. Unless the Special Instructions in this Power of Attorney state otherwise, you must also:

(a) Act loyally for the principal's benefit;

(b) Avoid conflicts that would impair your ability to act in the principal's best interest;

(c) Act with care, competence, and diligence;

(d) Keep a record of all receipts, disbursements and transactions made on behalf of the principal;

(e) Cooperate with any person that has authority to make health care decisions for the principal to do what you know the principal reasonably expects or, if you do not know the principal's expectations, to act in the principal's best interest; and

(f) Attempt to preserve the principal's estate plan if you know the plan and preserving the plan is consistent with the principal's best interest.

3. Termination of Agent's Authority. You must stop acting on behalf of the principal if you learn of any event that terminates this Power of Attorney or your authority under this Power of Attorney. Events that terminate a Power of Attorney or your authority to act under a Power of Attorney include:

(a) Death of the principal;

(b) The principal's revocation of the Power of Attorney or your authority;

(c) The occurrence of a termination event stated in the Power of Attorney;

(d) The purpose of the Power of Attorney is fully accomplished; or

(e) If you are married to the principal, your marriage is dissolved.

4. Liability of Agent. The meaning of the authority granted to you is defined in NRS 162A.200 to 162A.660, inclusive. If you violate NRS 162A.200 to 162A.660, inclusive, or act outside the authority granted in this Power of Attorney, you may be liable for any damages caused by your violation.

5. If there is anything about this document or your duties that you do not understand, you should seek legal advice.

CHAPTER 16
FORM 10: TEMPORARY GUARDIANSHIP

FORM LETS PARENT GIVE POWER TO SOMEONE OVER CHILD UNDER 18

This form lets a parent or similar with a child under age 18 name someone to have power to make decisions about a child. Some people call this the Short Term Guardianship or 6 Month Guardianship form. This book's form is a form used in Washoe County and most counties (a few counties have very minor differences). Clark County has a form with a couple different sentences and people there may want to search for and use this form. Many counties or legal aid groups have this form online so it can be filled in online and then printed.

FORM CAN GIVE BROAD POWER OVER A CHILD UNDER 18

This form lets a parent name someone as Temporary Guardian to make decisions about a child under 18 including on health care, school, home, discipline, food, and travel. This form can help if someone is caring for a child while a child and parent are apart for work, school, drug treatment, sports, prison or jail, military, immigration, long visit with family or friends, or if a child is in hospital and quick decisions needed. The form is usually not done for minor events like babysitting, daycare, short visits, or really any time a parent can come quickly. A person who signed the form can overrule a decision, fire the Guardian, or take back a child at any time. The form only has power for 6 months but can be renewed multiple times. This form does not involve a court at all. Parents mostly still have power over the child so really power is shared, and most schools or doctors will obey a parent who disagrees with the Temporary Guardian. Some health care providers may not accept the form so a Full Guardianship gotten at court may be needed. Most states have similar forms but may call it a "Power of Attorney Delegating Parental Authority" or similar.

FORM MUST BE SIGNED BY PEOPLE WITH A NOTARY

The form must be signed by 1 parent in front of a person who is a notary who then notarizes the form. A child 14 or older must sign though no notary is needed. Usually the 2nd parent of a child also must sign the form in a second spot though no notary is needed, but schools and doctors often do not check for this. The Temporary Guardian must sign at the end of the form using a notary who then notarizes the form. Once signed some extra cautious people quickly show it to schools and doctors in advance to explain how they should later follow it. Schools may have a form for a Temporary Guardian to register with the school. Either the parent who did the form, the Temporary Guardian, or a court can end things at any time by giving written notice by hand or mail to parents or Temporary Guardian, like: "This notice informs recipient the Temporary Guardianship has been terminated involving the child named _____. Date: ___ Signed:____".

SIX MONTH TEMPORARY GUARDIANSHIP UNDER CHAPTER 159A OF THE NEVADA REVISED STATUTES

I, (*parent name*) _____,

of (*address, city, state, zip code*) _____

the parent of the minor child, (*child's name*) _____

whose date of birth is_____, hereby desire to appoint

(*guardian's name*) _____

of (*address, city, state, zip code*)_____

as short term guardian pursuant to Chapter 159A of the Nevada Revised Statutes.

Carefully read each of the following statements and initial all that are true.

_____ 1. I am the legal custodian of the minor child.

_____ 2. The other parent's parental rights have not been terminated by court order.

_____ 3. The other parent's whereabouts are known.

_____ 4. The other parent is willing and able to make and carry out daily child care decisions concerning the minor child.

WARNING: *If paragraphs 2, 3, and 4 have all been initialed, the other parent must sign page 2 of this form to make this short-term guardianship valid.*

    I specifically consent that the named guardian may make whatever decisions are necessary concerning the day-to-day care of (*child's name*)_____, including educational decisions, legal decisions and health decisions. The named guardian may authorize all routine medical and dental care, and in the event of any medical emergency, the named guardian may authorize operative care.

    This guardianship shall expire six (6) months from the date that appears below unless it is renewed by an acknowledged writing prior to the expiration date. This guardianship may be terminated by me, by the guardian or by an order of a court of competent jurisdiction that may appoint a guardian of the minor child, but such termination must be accomplished by a written instrument.

    I am the legal custodian of the minor child and am competent to make this appointment.

Date: _____   Parent's Signature: _____

                          Print Your Name: _____

STATE OF _____

COUNTY OF _____

This instrument was acknowledged before me on

this _____ day of _____, _____ by _____.

_____.

NOTARY PUBLIC

PARENT'S CONSENT

I hereby consent to the above-named person being appointed as my child's guardian. I declare under penalty of perjury under the law of the State of Nevada that the foregoing is true and correct.

Date: _____   Parent's Signature: _____
                                        Print Your Name: _____

MINOR'S CONSENT

I hereby consent to the above-named person being appointed as my guardian.

Date: _____   Minor's Signature: _____
                                        Print Your Name: _____

GUARDIAN'S ACCEPTANCE OF APPOINTMENT

I, (*guardian's name*) _____ hereby accept this appointment as temporary short term guardian for the minor child identified in this instrument and will accept responsibility for the care, custody, and control of said minor child, including all necessary authority and power to furnish and provide care and services to said minor child as may seem necessary, proper, or desirable in the child's best interest and welfare, including, but not limited to, food, clothing, shelter, education, and medical-surgical-dental care and treatment. I understand this guardianship shall become effective upon my execution of this document in the presence of a Notary Public for a period of six (6) months and may be terminated by an instrument in writing signed by either parent of the minor child if that parent has not had their rights legally terminated by an order of a court of competent jurisdiction.

Date: _____   Guardian's Signature: _____
                                        Print Your Name: _____

STATE OF _____
COUNTY OF _____

This instrument was acknowledged before me on

this _____ day of _____, _____ by _____.

_____.
NOTARY PUBLIC

CHAPTER 17
FORM 11: AFFIDAVIT AUTHORIZING PERSON TO ORDER BURIAL OR CREMATION

FORM LETS A PERSON BE NAMED TO CONTROL BODILY REMAINS

This form lets a person later control their dead body (their "remains") by naming someone to control this and make suggestions. This is a statutory form found in state law with blank lines added to put suggestions.

CAN NAME PERSON TO CONTROL BODILY REMAINS

The form lets to someone be authorized to later control burial, cremation, and any related issues. This form is allowed by Nevada Revised Statutes 451.024, which says

"A person 18 years of age or older wishing to authorize another person to order the burial or cremation of his or her human remains in the event of the person's death may include such an authorization in a validly executed will or durable power of attorney or may execute an affidavit before a notary public[.]"

If this form is not done by then law control is by closest family (spouse, children, parents, then siblings). People do this form rarely, usually if it seems family may be too upset while mourning, be bad with money, or do unwanted things. Payment for things comes from pre-paid funeral accounts, insurance, and a dead person's or estate's money and property, and Executor and family are legally required to help arrange payment with these. In general by law people including family should help do the funeral, burial, and related things the dead person wanted if their properly, money, and estate can afford it. The form has an area to tell people things but many people skip this and trust a person named or family to do what was discussed. Note, a person can also control their bodily remains in a Will or other legal documents.

SEVERAL OPTIONS ABOUT WHAT TO DO WITH BODILY REMAINS

What to do with bodily remains when someone dies can be complicated. Basically, after a death police are told and then a funeral home or crematorium come get the body. Roughly half of people pick burial and half cremation. If picking cremation later "cremains" go to family or a "columbarium" vault in cemetery.

Half of people do not do early events in first month when shocked family may be unready for visitors. Importantly, if "Direct Burial" or "Direct Cremation" is requested costs may be 80% off the usual prices but this skips events with body till burial or cremation in done with no family involvement. Weeks later people may do ash scattering, ceremony, or dinner at park, house, church, or hall, often with food, speech, or video.

Half of people do early events within month, and there are many options for a person to pick from. First, some people do within days a "Vigil", "Viewing", or "Wake", where family and friends talk or just pray maybe in room with body (closed or open casket) or cremated ashes, often at Funeral Home or church. Second, some people do big ceremony within week of either a) funeral (maybe with Mass) in church with priest or minister, or b) informal event like "Celebration of Life" or "Remembrance" with or without the body. Third, some people do final event at cemetery (religious or not), like a burial or putting ashes in a vault.

SIGN FORM WITH NOTARY

To complete form it is signed by person in front of a notary who then notarizes it. Once done the form should be given to someone to hold or put in a place it can be found very quickly within days of a death.

AFFIDAVIT AUTHORIZING PERSON TO ORDER BURIAL OR CREMATION

(Nevada Revised Statutes § 451.024)

State of Nevada   }
                                   } ss

County of _____   }

(Date) _____

I, _____, (person authorizing another person to order the burial or cremation of his or her human remains in the event of his or her death) do hereby designate _____ (person who is being authorized to order the burial or cremation of the human remains of a person in the event of his or her death) to order the disposition of my human remains upon my death.

I also wish to tell the person who is being authorized the following but this does not in any way limit their power to order or do anything:

_____

_____

_____

_____

_____

_____

_____

_____

_____

_____

Subscribed and sworn to before me this ___ day of the month of _____ of the year _____.

_____
(Notary Public)

APPENDIX: SAMPLE FILLED OUT FORMS

TO GET FORMS TO USE PEOPLE CAN:

(1) PHOTOCOPY BOOK PAGES,

(2) TEAR OUT PAGES FROM A BOOK, OR

(3) DOWNLOAD BOOK WITH FORMS FROM WWW.DAVENPORTPUBLISHING.COM AND USUALLY PDF FORM AT IS BEST TO AVOID SPACING/FORMAT CHANGES, AND THEN PEOPLE JUST HANDWRITE ON THE PRINTED OUT DOCUMENT.

EMAIL ANY COMMENTS TO DAVENPORTPRESS@GMAIL.COM.

On the next pages to show how it can be done are some sample filled out legal forms.

People can add words to legal forms by computer or typewriter to be neater, but many people just by hand use pen, marker, or pencil to handwrite words into forms.

It is not required but is bit better if signatures are in ink or marker not pencil.

Many parts of the forms especially Will gifts can be left empty and unfilled.

Anyone can fill in words in legal form not just the person doing the form, like a friend with neat writing can fill in all the words, addresses, and dates that are needed. Only the final signatures must be done by each person who wants the form.

To add words in form by pen, pencil, typewriter, or computer any of these is fine:
"I appoint ___*John Doe*___ as Agent" ,
"I appoint ___John Doe___ as Agent",
"I appoint John Doe as Agent".

When doing forms it may help to know "respectively" means "in order just stated".

People need not worry about neatness or small mistakes, and a document is usually fine if those people who knew a decedent in life can tell the likely meaning.

LAST WILL AND TESTAMENT

I, *Paul Thomas Maxwell* , of *Clark* County, Nevada, do revoke all prior Wills, Testaments, and Codicils, and do make, publish, and declare this as my Will. I am of sound mind and under no duress or undue influence and acting voluntarily.

1. GIFTS. I give these gifts in this Will, but to get a gift in this section the recipient must survive me except as otherwise stated below.

I give _____ to _____.

I give _____ to _____.

I give _____ to _____.

I give _____ to _____.

I give _____ to _____.

I give _____ to _____.

I give _____ to _____.

2. SEPARATE WRITINGS. I may do writings separate from this Will to gift tangible personal property as allowed by state law including Nevada Revised Statutes 133.045 and such writings should be followed. This Will does not revoke any such writings that exist. A gift in such a writing to a person who does not survive me is canceled and has no effect. Any such writing not found within 90 days of my death is canceled and has no effect.

3. RESIDUE. I give the rest and residue and remainder of my estate, my money and property of any kind and nature, and anything I have an interest in so long as it was not transferred by other Will provisions (all of which is called the "residue"), as follows:

a) to *Susan Lee Maxwell* who survive me with persons just named who survive me taking the share of non-survivors, then

b) to *Oscar David Maxwell and Jennifer Judy Tabor* and if any of those just named do not survive me their part goes to their lineal descendants, per stirpes.

4. ADMINISTRATION. I name and appoint *Susan Lee Maxwell* as Personal Representative including for me, my Will, and my estate.

5. MISCELLANEOUS.

5. MISCELLANEOUS. The following applies to this Will and generally.

Nevada is my primary residence and its laws should apply to this Will.

Priority of Will gifts of the same type is based on the order they are written.

In this document no unfilled part is a mistake and residue spaces may be left blank.

The words "give" and "gift" also means a devise, bequest, grant, legacy, or similar.

A gift of property no longer owned by Testator at death shall lapse and be of no effect including no payment of money shall be done in its place, all without ademption.

If a gift or section reasonably mentions survival in any way then survival is an absolute condition and anti-lapse laws or similar have no effect.

Unless a Will gift specifies otherwise if a Will gift goes to multiple recipients if any do not survive Testator their part lapses and the remaining part passes to surviving recipients.

Any failure to make more or any Will gifts to current children or current spouse at the time I do this Will is intentional and not a mistake to remedy.

No gift or transfer I made during my life reduces or offsets a Will gift unless during my life I expressly usually called it a "loan" or "advancement".

Unless another meaning is clearly shown by context use of plural includes the singular and vice versa, and masculine, feminine and neuter words are used interchangeably. Unless another meaning is shown "they" means both one person and multiple persons.

Unless a Will says otherwise a secured debt like mortgage or lien shall not be paid off, recipient of a Will gift of property takes it subject to any debts, and no such recipient who later loses the property to a debtor or who pays a debtor to avoid foreclosure or other loss may require the estate, heirs, devisees, or others to pay recipient back or do anything.

I request and authorize any informal, summary, and quick probate or similar action. Any Personal Representative may act independently with no supervision of any court or similar thing, including independent administration, and with action or filings in court.

I give any Personal Representative a) the fullest authority, powers, and discretion allowed by state law, b) authority to lease, sell, mortgage, convey, or retain property including real property in any such manner and time they deem helpful or proper, and c) authority to anytime settle or pay claims or debts they in their sole discretion choose. Any Personal Representative shall also have all powers found in Nevada Revised Statutes existing on the date of this Will and any other powers hereafter conferred by law.

A Personal Representative shall have sole discretion how to balance people's feelings and pick property or divide a gift to carry out a general gift or a gift to multiple persons.

If context permits the terms Personal Representative, Administrator, and Executor are interchangeable as if all were written, and Conservator is interchangeable with Guardian of the Estate and Guardian of Property. The term Residue also means Residuary.

I request any lawyers be paid hourly or as agreed and not by percentage fee schedule.

The residue includes lapsed or failed gifts, insurance paid to estate, inheritances owed me, and property I had or have a power of appointment or testamentary disposition over.

Any Personal Representative, Executor, Administrator, Guardian of any type, Conservator, Custodian, and any fiduciary under this Will or otherwise shall qualify and serve without bond, security, surety, or any similar thing.

If part of this Will is by law invalid or unenforceable other provisions remain in effect.

Any Personal Representative in their sole discretion may at any time transfer money or property of a minor under age 18 to a Custodian under Nevada's Uniform Act on Transfers to Minors law or any similar law anywhere. The Custodian holding money and property can make discretionary payments of any kind and to any recipient to benefit the minor, and later pay any remainder to a minor at age 18. When doing this no bond, court action, or anything is required. Any Personal Representative may select the Custodian including themselves but if they do not I name for this the Guardian of the Estate named in this Will.

TESTATOR

I, as Testator of this Will, do now declare, publish, and sign this instrument as my Will this this _22nd_ day of _June_ , 20_22_.

Paul Thomas Maxwell
Testator signature

DECLARATION OF WITNESSES

Under penalty of perjury pursuant to the law of the State of Nevada, the undersigned, _Eve Mable Rogers_ and _Mary Ann Moon_ , declare that the following is true of their own knowledge: That they witnessed the execution of the foregoing Will of the Testator, _Paul Thomas Maxwell_ ; that the Testator subscribed the Will and declared it to be his or her last Will and testament in their presence; that they thereafter subscribed the Will as witnesses in the presence of the Testator and in the presence of each other and at the request of the Testator; and that the Testator at the time of the execution of the Will appeared to them to be of full age and of sound mind and memory.

Dated this _22nd_ day of _June_ , 20_22_.

Eve Mable Rogers   _14 2nd St., Las Vegas, NV, 89103_
Witness   Witness Address

Mary Ann Moon   _83 Buffalo Road, Milwaukee, WI 53290_
Witness   Witness Address

LAST WILL AND TESTAMENT

I, _____Mary Kathleen Kent_____, of ____Tucson____, Nevada, do revoke all prior Wills, Testaments, and Codicils, and do make, publish, and declare this as my Will. I am of sound mind and under no duress or undue influence and acting voluntarily.

1. GIFTS. I give these gifts in this Will, but to get a gift in this section the recipient must survive me except as otherwise stated below.

I give _big oak table_ to _Anne J. Wix._

I give ___$500___ to ___Loretta Marsha Switt_.

I give __63 Ivy Road, Henderson, Nevada__ to _Kenneth Victor Poppler._

I give _all real property I own in Washoe County, Nevada_ to _Greta Olivia Fox_.

I give _903 Iceberg Road, Anchorage, Alaska_ to _James Eric Hanson_.

I give _Bronze Roman Lamp_ to _Anne Kilby_ and _Kevin Kilby._

I give _blue blanket_ to _Ruth Jones._

I give _all blankets not given above_ to _Kay Pidoski._

I give _Wells Fargo acct ending in #8923_ to _Wendy Deer a childhood friend_.

I give _1998 Ford truck_ to _John Rupert Smith_.

I give _$200_ to _Binker Food Shelf on Smith Road in Las Vegas, Nevada_.

I give _all spare tires and auto parts I own_ to _Victor Perez my mechanic_.

I give ___$100 each___ to _each of my cousins_.

2. SEPARATE WRITINGS. I may do writings separate from this Will to gift tangible personal property as allowed by state law including Nevada Revised Statutes 133.045 and such writings should be followed. This Will does not revoke any such writings that exist. A gift in such a writing to a person who does not survive me is canceled and has no effect. Any such writing not found within 90 days of my death is canceled and has no effect.

3. RESIDUE. I give the rest and residue and remainder of my estate, my property of any kind and nature, and anything I have an interest in (all of which is called the "residue"), so long as any such thing was not transferred by other Will provisions, as follows:

   a) to _____John Abraham Kent my husband_____ who survive me with persons just named who survive me taking the share of non-survivors, then

   b) to _45% to Oscar Elliot Kent my son and 45% to Karen Lisa Lundy my daughter and 10% to Ana Juanita Sanchez my niece_ and if any of those just named do not survive me their part goes to their lineal descendants, per stirpes.

4. ADMINISTRATION. I name and appoint _John Abraham Kent_ as Personal Representative including for me, my Will, and my estate.

5. GUARDIAN. I name to serve when proper _Karen Lisa Fox my sister_ as Guardian of the Person with control, authority, and custody of any minor child, and also as Guardian of the Estate with control and authority over any minor child's property, money, and estate

6. MISCELLANEOUS. The following applies to this Will and generally.

   Nevada is my primary residence and its laws should apply to this Will.

   Priority of Will gifts of the same type is based on the order they are written.

   In this document no unfilled part is a mistake and residue spaces may be left blank.

   The words "give" and "gift" also means a devise, bequest, grant, legacy, or similar.

   A gift of property no longer owned by Testator at death shall lapse and be of no effect including no payment of money shall be done in its place, all without ademption.

   If a gift or section reasonably mentions survival in any way then survival is an absolute condition and anti-lapse laws or similar have no effect.

   Unless a Will gift specifies otherwise if a Will gift goes to multiple recipients if any do not survive Testator their part lapses and the remaining part passes to surviving recipients.

   Any failure to make more or any Will gifts to current children or current spouse at the time I do this Will is intentional and not a mistake to remedy.

   No gift or transfer I made during my life reduces or offsets a Will gift unless during my life I expressly usually called it a "loan" or "advancement".

   Unless another meaning is clearly shown by context use of plural includes the singular and vice versa, and masculine, feminine and neuter words are used interchangeably. Unless another meaning is shown "they" means both one person and multiple persons.

   I request and authorize any informal, summary, and quick probate or similar action. Any Personal Representative may act independently with no supervision of any court or similar thing, including independent administration, and with action or filings in court.

   A Personal Representative shall have sole discretion how to balance people's feelings and pick property or divide a gift to carry out a general gift or a gift to multiple persons.

If context permits the terms Personal Representative, Administrator, and Executor are interchangeable as if all were written, and Conservator is interchangeable with Guardian of the Estate and Guardian of Property. The term Residue also means Residuary.

I request any lawyers be paid hourly or as agreed and not by percentage fee schedule.

The residue includes lapsed or failed gifts, insurance paid to estate, inheritances owed me, and property I had or have a power of appointment or testamentary disposition over.

Any Personal Representative, Executor, Administrator, Guardian of any type, Conservator, Custodian, and any fiduciary under this Will or otherwise shall qualify and serve without bond, security, surety, or any similar thing.

If part of this Will is by law invalid or unenforceable other provisions remain in effect.

Any Personal Representative in their sole discretion may at any time transfer money or property of a minor under age 18 to a Custodian under Nevada's Uniform Act on Transfers to Minors law or any similar law anywhere. The Custodian holding money and property can make discretionary payments of any kind and to any recipient to benefit the minor, and later pay any remainder to a minor at age 18. When doing this no bond, court action, or anything is required. Any Personal Representative may select the Custodian including themselves but if they do not I name for this the Guardian of the Estate named in this Will.

TESTATOR

I, as Testator of this Will, do now declare, publish, and sign this instrument as my Will this 30th day of December , 20 19.

Mary Kathleen Kent
Testator signature

DECLARATION OF WITNESSES

Under penalty of perjury pursuant to the law of the State of Nevada, the undersigned, Olivia Joy Pawlenty and Roy Felix Pawlenty , declare that the following is true of their own knowledge: That they witnessed the execution of the foregoing Will of the Testator, Mary Kathleen Kent ; that the Testator subscribed the Will and declared it to be his or her last Will and testament in their presence; that they thereafter subscribed the Will as witnesses in the presence of the Testator and in the presence of each other and at the request of the Testator; and that the Testator at the time of the execution of the Will appeared to them to be of full age and of sound mind and memory.

Dated this 30th day of December , 20 19.

Olivia Joy Pawlenty	87 Henderson Avenue, Las Vegas, NV 89054
Witness	Witness Address

Roy Felix Pawlenty	87 Henderson Avenue, Las Vegas, NV 89054
Witness	Witness Address

LAST WILL AND TESTAMENT

I, **David Eric Smith**, of **Washoe** County, Nevada, do revoke all of my prior Wills, Testaments, and Codicils, and do make, publish, and declare this as my Will.

I am of sound mind and under no duress or undue influence and acting voluntarily.

1. GIFTS. I give these gifts in this Will, but to get a gift in this section the recipient must survive me except as otherwise stated below.

I give ____$500____ to _each of my brothers, sisters, and cousins_____ .

I give ____$1000____ to _First Bethel Food Pantry, Reno, Nevada_____ .

2. SEPARATE WRITINGS. I may do writings separate from this Will to gift tangible personal property as allowed by state law including Nevada Revised Statutes 133.045 and such writings should be followed. This Will does not revoke any such writings that exist. A gift in such a writing to a person who does not survive me is canceled and has no effect. Any such writing not found within 90 days of my death is canceled and has no effect.

3. RESIDUE. The rest and residue and remainder of my estate, my property of any kind and nature, and anything I have an interest in, I give to **Adam Michael Smith and Ann Sue Baker who survive me** and to lineal descendants per stirpes of a person just named who did not survive me.

4. ADMINISTRATION. I name and appoint **Ann Sue Baker** as Personal Representative including for me, my Will, and my estate.

5. MISCELLANEOUS. The following applies to this Will and generally.

Nevada is my primary residence and its laws should apply to this Will.

Priority of Will gifts of the same type is based on the order they are written.

In this document no unfilled part is a mistake and residue spaces may be left blank.

The words "give" and "gift" also means a devise, bequest, grant, legacy, or similar.

A gift of property no longer owned by Testator at death shall lapse and be of no effect including no payment of money shall be done in its place, all without ademption.

If a gift or section reasonably mentions survival in any way then survival is an absolute condition and anti-lapse laws or similar have no effect.

Unless a Will gift specifies otherwise if a Will gift goes to multiple recipients if any do

not survive Testator their part lapses and the remaining part passes to surviving recipients.

Any failure to make more or any Will gifts to current children or current spouse at the time I do this Will is intentional and not a mistake to remedy.

No gift or transfer I made during my life reduces or offsets a Will gift unless during my life I expressly usually called it a "loan" or "advancement".

Unless another meaning is clearly shown by context use of plural includes the singular and vice versa, and masculine, feminine and neuter words are used interchangeably. Unless another meaning is shown "they" means both one person and multiple persons.

Unless a Will says otherwise a secured debt like mortgage or lien shall not be paid off, recipient of a Will gift of property takes it subject to any debts, and no such recipient who later loses the property to a debtor or who pays a debtor to avoid foreclosure or other loss may require the estate, heirs, devisees, or others to pay recipient back or do anything.

I request and authorize any informal, summary, and quick probate or similar action. Any Personal Representative may act independently with no supervision of any court or similar thing, including independent administration, and with action or filings in court.

I give any Personal Representative a) the fullest authority, powers, and discretion allowed by state law, b) authority to lease, sell, mortgage, convey, or retain property including real property in any such manner and time they deem helpful or proper, and c) authority to anytime settle or pay claims or debts they in their sole discretion choose. Any Personal Representative shall also have all powers found in Nevada Revised Statutes existing on the date of this Will and any other powers hereafter conferred by law.

A Personal Representative shall have sole discretion how to balance people's feelings and pick property or divide a gift to carry out a general gift or a gift to multiple persons.

If context permits the terms Personal Representative, Administrator, and Executor are interchangeable as if all were written, and Conservator is interchangeable with Guardian of the Estate and Guardian of Property. The term Residue also means Residuary.

I request any lawyers be paid hourly or as agreed and not by percentage fee schedule.

The residue includes lapsed or failed gifts, insurance paid to estate, inheritances owed me, and property I had or have a power of appointment or testamentary disposition over.

Any Personal Representative, Executor, Administrator, Guardian of any type, Conservator, Custodian, and any fiduciary under this Will or otherwise shall qualify and serve without bond, security, surety, or any similar thing.

If part of this Will is by law invalid or unenforceable other provisions remain in effect.

Any Personal Representative in their sole discretion may at any time transfer money or property of a minor under age 18 to a Custodian under Nevada's Uniform Act on Transfers to Minors law or any similar law anywhere. The Custodian holding money and property can make discretionary payments of any kind and to any recipient to benefit the minor, and later pay any remainder to a minor at age 18. When doing this no bond, court action, or anything is required. Any Personal Representative may select the Custodian including themselves but if they do not I name for this the Guardian of the Estate named in this Will.

TESTATOR

I, as Testator of this Will, do now declare, publish, and sign this instrument as my Will this **21st** day of **June**, 2021.

David Eric Smith
_____
Testator signature

DECLARATION OF WITNESSES

Under penalty of perjury pursuant to the law of the State of Nevada, the undersigned, **Harriet Potter** and **Pamela Bonnie Jones**, declare that the following is true of their own knowledge: That they witnessed the execution of the foregoing Will of the Testator, **David Eric Smith**; that the Testator subscribed the Will and declared it to be his or her last Will and testament in their presence; that they thereafter subscribed the Will as witnesses in the presence of the Testator and in the presence of each other and at the request of the Testator; and that the Testator at the time of the execution of the Will appeared to them to be of full age and of sound mind and memory.

Dated this **21st** day of **June**, 2021.

Harriet Potter
_____
Witness signature

204 Pike Street, Washoe City, NV 89126
_____
Witness address

Pamela Bonnie Jones
_____
Witness signature

27 Columbia Road, Boulder City, NV 89035
_____
Witness address

SELF-PROVING AFFIDAVIT

State of Nevada   }

                               }ss.

County of __*Washoe*__   }

(Date) _June 21, 2021_

Then and there personally appeared __*Harriet Potter*__ and __*Pamela Bonnie Jones*__ who, being duly sworn, depose and say: That they witnessed the execution of the foregoing will of the Testator, __*David Eric Smith*__ ; that the Testator subscribed the will and declared it to be his or her last Will and testament in their presence; that they thereafter subscribed the Will as witnesses in the presence of the Testator and in the presence of each other and at the request of the Testator; and that the Testator at the time of the execution of the Will appeared to them to be of full age and of sound mind and memory.

Harriet Potter
Affiant

Pamela Bonnie Jones
Affiant

Subscribed and sworn to before me this
_21st_ day of the month of __*June*__ of the year _2021_.

Jane T. Dodd
Notary Public

JANE T. DODD
NOTARY PUBLIC
STATE OF NEVADA
Appt. No. 97-1409-7
My Appt. Expires May 8, 2029

TANGIBLE PERSONAL PROPERTY LIST

This writing is referred to in my Will and gives tangible personal property at my death as allowed by state law including by Nevada Revised Statutes 133.045. I may do multiple pages like this which all should be followed with the more recent controlling any conflicts. Any page not found within 90 days of my death is canceled. If a person getting a gift below does not survive me a gift to them is canceled.

PROPERTY ITEMS		NAMES OF RECIPIENTS
1998 Ford Truck	to	Samantha Bell
1.3 carat diamond ring + Irish rings	to	Ann Sue Reed
14 ft power boat + kayak + paddles	to	L. Wheeler
Amish style bench	to	Reba Stewart
glass table, telescope, umbrellas	to	Rebecca Stewart
Irish wood cups, oak platter, red vase	to	Mary and Cindy Lott
painting of sailboat in storm	to	Mary Lott
chainsaw marked with 382937	to	Mary Lott
chainsaw marked with 89930	to	Matt Smith
antique lanterns + repair kits	to	Sue Wu waitress at cafe
oak lamp with big scratch	to	Mary Kay Poppler
sewing machines	to	Mary Kay Poppler
rocking chair bought in Montana	to	Don Winkler boat mechanic
all fishing poles and fishing nets	to	Joe "Fish" Hoss, fishing pal
hats at cabin	to	Ken Baker
	to	
	to	
	to	
	to	

DATE: 2-12-2023   SIGNED: *David Eric Smith*